P9-CRM-237

QUILTS, QUILTS, AND MORE QUILTS!

Diana McClun
and
Laura Nownes

C&T PUBLISHING

Copyright © 1993 Diana McClun and Laura Nownes

Edited by Harold Nadel
Technical editing by Elizabeth Aneloski and Barbara Kuhn
Design by Kajun Graphics, San Francisco
Computer graphics by Kandy Petersen, Moraga, California
Photography by Sharon Risedorph, San Francisco
Back cover photograph by Tim Westhoven, Bowling Green, Ohio
Typographical composition by DC Typography, San Francisco
Draft editing by Sue Bowen

Homes graciously lent for photography by Stevan & Stephany Cavalier and Neil &
    Freddy Moran
Photography styled by Adrian Gallardo & Renee Isabelle Walker, Stephen Reed
    Flowers, Lafayette, California

The authors wish to thank Bernina of America and Fairfield Processing
    Corporation.
Sewing assistance by Sandi Klop and Julie Shirley Murphy
Original patterns graciously lent by Mary Ellen Hopkins and Freddy Moran

▼▼▼

The authors dedicate this book lovingly to their dedicated husbands.

ISBN 0-914881-67-1

All rights reserved. No part of this work covered by the copyright hereon may be
reproduced or used in any form or by any means—graphic, electronic, or
mechanical, including photocopying, recording, taping, or information storage
and retrieval system—without written permission of the publisher.

The copyrights on individual works are retained by the artists.

Library of Congress Cataloging-in-Publication Data
McClun, Diana,
        Quilts, quilts, and more quilts!   Diana McClun and Laura Nownes.
        p.   cm.
      ISBN 0-914881-67-1
        1. Quilting—Patterns.   2. Patchwork—Patterns.   3. Appliqué—Patterns.
    I. Nownes, Laura.   II. Title.
    TT835.M3993   1993
    746.9'7—dc20
                                                            93-28345
                                                            CIP

Published by C & T Publishing
P.O. Box 1456
Lafayette, California 94549

Printed in Hong Kong

10 9 8 7 6 5 4 3 2 1

CONTENTS

▼▼▼*Chapter 6*
QUILTING

▼▼▼*Chapter 7*
BINDING

INTRODUCTION

Quiltmakers are always on the lookout for simple, wonderful patterns, new fabric designs, and setting and border ideas in classically traditional styles. Our love of quilts and teaching inspired us to put together this book, in order to share many of the new quilts we have made. We have included new ideas for making them using quick-cutting and piecing techniques.

Our first book, *Quilts! Quilts!! Quilts!!!*, is enjoying its fifth year in print, and *Quilts Galore!* its third. In *Quilts, Quilts, and More Quilts!*, we have interwoven the best aspects of both earlier books, presenting different patterns, updated fabrics, and new techniques. With simplicity in mind, we have tried to take the complexity out of quiltmaking while conveying the spirit of creativity.

We are excited about these new quilts and have worked hard to make each one unique, starting with familiar, traditional patterns, but giving each one new life with the choices of fabrics, settings, and borders. The designs are especially appealing because they appear to be more complex than they truly are. Each pattern was selected with the requirement that it must be easy enough for a quiltmaker at any level of experience. Practiced quiltmakers will be challenged and inspired to try some of the new ideas and stretch their skills.

In the final production of this book, we both had to agree on and like the quilts. During the planning stages it was pointed out to us that we had an abundance of red quilts. Of course, red is Laura's favorite color, and Diana loves it as well. Even though red fills our souls, we needed to consider our readers' tastes, so we eliminated three of the red quilts and added the blue and white *Garden Maze*.

Our own homes are filled with quilts: some we made ourselves, some we collected, and some we received as gifts; all are filled with special stories and memories. We use our quilts daily, and we want you to feel comfortable about using them as bed covers, tablecloths, picnic cloths, sofa and chair covers, about hanging them on banisters and out windows.

We know that many of you use the sampler quilts from our other books as learning tools. You have asked for more ideas and specific instructions for making them. In this book we have devoted an entire chapter to sampler quilts, allowing you to savor each block individually. Understanding the shapes, sewing them in a convenient order, with helpful hints and practice exercises, will help you to construct the quilts. Most of the quilts in Chapter 1 have block designs that can also be incorporated into a sampler quilt. We invited Katie, Sandy, and Sally, three quiltmaking instructors, to test our patterns; they produced glorious samplers, so different and so individual in their focus on color, techniques, and settings. The purpose of a textbook is to allow you to teach yourself the skill of interrelating different patterns and styles without appearing haphazard. We are instructors ourselves, and we know the value of having a textbook. We have therefore included a class outline for an eleven-week in-depth study. We hope this book succeeds as a text for quiltmaking, as a guide to fabric choices and color, and as fuel in the process of putting a successful quilt together from start to binding.

Quilts keep our personal environments alive. As you browse the photographs, note the dazzling array of patterns and colors, and you will be enticed to make several of the breathtaking quilts immediately. Let yourself be captivated by the wonder of quilts. When the eye is pleased, the soul is fed. We hope you share our excitement and continue to add to your collection of quilts, quilts, and more quilts!

—*Diana and Laura*

Chapter 1

▼▼▼

PATTERNS

This chapter includes twenty-eight quilt patterns; many are traditional and familiar patterns, but some are new and original. They are presented in a logical sequence, from the easiest to the more challenging and time-consuming.

Each pattern includes:

• A color photo of a quilt made from the pattern. The number of blocks in the sample quilt does not necessarily correspond with any of the wall or bed sizes given.

• Block size: the finished size, without seam allowance. Your individual completed blocks should measure ½″ larger than the block size indicated.

• Setting indicates whether the blocks are sewn together in straight horizontal and vertical rows (straight setting) or turned on point and sewn in diagonal rows (diagonal setting). Instructions for both are given in Chapter 5.

• A line diagram of an individual block, showing suggested light, medium, and dark color placement.

• Finished quilt sizes for a variety of wall and bed dimensions. The measurements have been rounded to the nearest whole numbers.

• Block setting, which indicates how the blocks are sewn together (number of blocks across and number of blocks down).

• Total number of blocks or units required for making the quilt, and the number of alternate blocks, or side triangles, if appropriate.

• A yardage chart indicating the amount of fabric needed to make the quilt in various wall and bed sizes. If the quilt has one or more borders, yardage is given for cutting the strips on either the crosswise or lengthwise grain of the fabric if you can save a significant amount of fabric by cutting crosswise. Otherwise, only lengthwise amounts are given. With the exception of the *Sawtooth* quilt, yardage for binding allows for a ¼″-wide finished binding. Refer to Chapter 7 for specific instructions on cutting fabric strips for the binding.

• A line diagram of the block, showing the individual shapes and indicating the template number for each one. Template patterns are found at the back of the book. Each one is given a number and a letter; for example, template pattern 6c can be found on the sixth page of the template patterns.

• Cutting instructions for both traditional and quick methods. The template patterns required for making the quilt are indicated for traditional cutting. The line diagram will assist you in determining the total number of shapes required for one block. If you are using quick-cutting methods, you will find the required number of strips or shapes to cut from each

fabric for the size quilt you are making. Cutting instructions for any sashing, borders, and backing immediately follow the quick-cutting chart. Backing instructions refer you to a diagram on page 144 which will assist you in piecing the lengths of backing fabric together.

• Construction section gives brief instructions and clear sequential sew order diagrams. NOTE: For clarity, diagrams do not include seam allowance.

Everything you need to make the quilts is here. We suggest you:

1. Choose a pattern from this chapter.

2. Decide on the size quilt you want to make. It is always best to measure your wall space or bed to determine if you want your finished quilt larger or smaller than the size suggested in the chart. Then you can make any necessary adjustments.

3. Select fabric and determine the amount to purchase, referring to the appropriate column in the yardage chart for help.

4. Prepare your fabric. See Chapter 4 for help.

5. Cut your fabric shapes, referring to the appropriate cutting chart, either traditional or quick.

6. Organize the cut shapes.

7. Construct the blocks using the sew order diagrams and referring to the techniques in Chapter 4.

FOUR-PATCH

3" block, straight set with alternate blocks

Diana McClun and Laura Nownes; quilted by Kathy Sandbach

▼

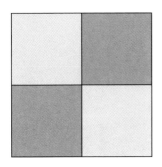

	CRIB/WALL	TWIN	DOUBLE/QUEEN	KING
Finished size	*48" x 60"*	*72" x 90"*	*90" x 96"*	*102" x 96"*
Blocks set	13 x 17	21 x 27	27 x 29	31 x 29
Pieced blocks	111	284	392	450
Alternate blocks	110	283	391	449
Pieced blocks (border)	68	104	120	128

YARDAGE ◀

	CRIB/WALL	TWIN	DOUBLE/QUEEN	KING
Pieced blocks, alternate blocks, and pieced border: fabrics to total*	3¼	7	8	10
Inner border:				
Crosswise	⅜	½	⅝	⅝
or Lengthwise	1⅝	2½	2⅝	2⅝
Backing	3	5½	8	8½
Binding	⅜	½	⅝	⅝

*See Helpful Hint in Step 1.

CUTTING ◀

TRADITIONAL:
Use template patterns 1b and 1d.

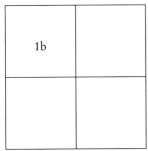

3" block

QUICK:	CRIB/WALL	TWIN	DOUBLE/QUEEN	KING
Pieced blocks and pieced border: 2"-wide strips	32	70	94	106
Alternate blocks: 3½"-wide strips	10	24	33	38
Cut strips to 3½" squares.				
BORDERS AND BACKING:				
Inner border: 2"-wide strips:				
Crosswise	6	8	9	10
or Lengthwise	4	4	4	4
Backing: lengths	2	2	3	3
See piecing diagram	B	A	D	C

▼

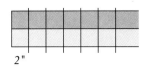

2"

Step 1

Step 2

1. Make the required number of pieced four-patch blocks: sew various combinations of strips together in pairs. Then cut the sets apart every 2", as shown.

✂ *HELPFUL HINT*: The sets can be layered for cutting if the seams are opposing on alternate sets. Since there are a variety of four-patch combinations, each requiring a different amount for the diagonal rows, it is helpful to make a quick sketch before joining strips to determine how many are needed of each combination. Each set of strips will make ten four-patch blocks.

2. Block sew order: see diagram.

3. Lay out all the blocks, alternating four-patch and alternate blocks. Each combination of four-patch blocks should form a diagonal row. Refer to the photo for help.

4. Sew all the blocks together in a straight set. Refer to Chapter 5 for specific instructions.

5. Sew the inner border to the quilt top.

6. Make the required number of pieced four-patch blocks for the border, using the techniques in Steps 1 and 2. Then join blocks to make the border. Each side requires one more four-patch than your original block set (5 x 7 set requires 6 x 8, plus corners), as shown.

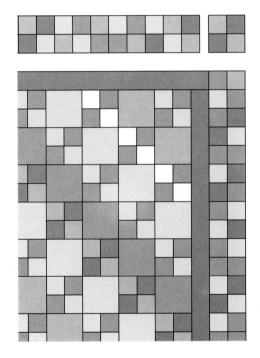

Steps 3–6

STRIPPED NINE-PATCH

6" block, straight set with vertical pieced sashing units and alternate blocks

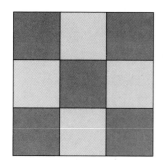

	CRIB/WALL	TWIN	DOUBLE/QUEEN	KING
Finished size	*42" x 54"*	*78" x 90"*	*96" x 90"*	*114" x 102"*
Blocks set	5 x 9	9 x 15	11 x 15	13 x 17
Pieced blocks	23	68	83	111
Alternate blocks	22	67	82	110
Sashing units	36	120	150	204

YARDAGE ◄

Pieced blocks and sashing units: fabrics to total	1¾	5⅜	6¾	8¾
Alternate blocks and binding	1¼	2⅞	3¼	4¼
Backing	1¾	5¼	8	9

CUTTING ◄

TRADITIONAL:
Use template patterns 1c, 1f, and 4i.

QUICK:

Pieced blocks: 2½"-wide strips	13	39	47	63
Sashing units: 1½"-wide strips	18	60	78	102
Alternate blocks: 6½"-wide strips	4	12	14	19
Cut strips to 6½" squares.				
Backing: lengths	1	2	3	3
See piecing diagram	—	A	C	C

6" block

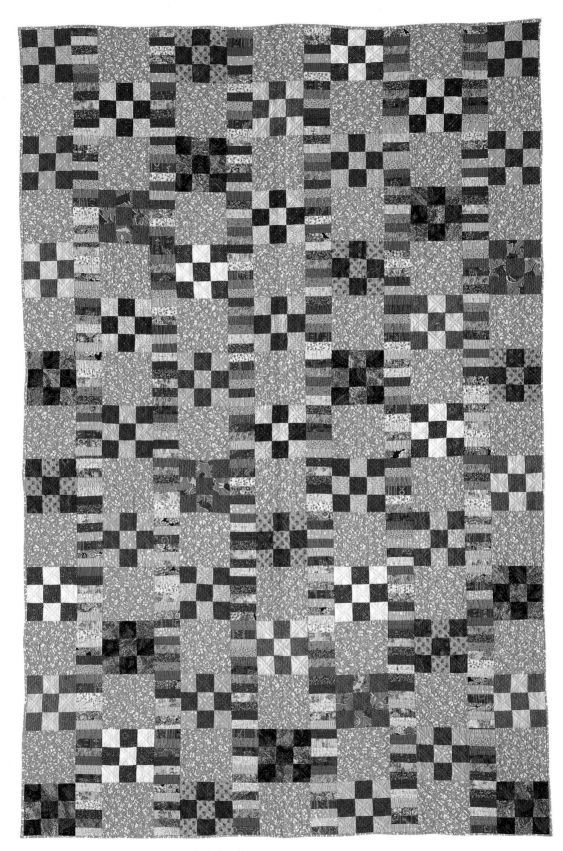

Emily Prindle, age 9; quilted by Anna Venti

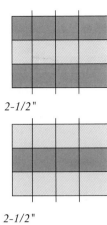

2-1/2"

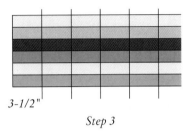

2-1/2"

Step 1

CONSTRUCTION

1. Make the required number of nine-patch blocks. Sew several different combinations of strips. Then cut the sets apart every 2½", as shown.

2. Sew order: see diagrams.

3. To make the pieced sashing units: sew the 1½"-wide strips together in sets of six. Then cut apart every 3½", as shown.

✄ *HELPFUL HINT*: Each set of strips will make twelve pieced sashing units.

4. Lay out the nine-patch blocks, pieced sashing units, and alternate blocks, as shown.

5. Sew the blocks together in a straight set. Refer to Chapter 5 for specific instructions.

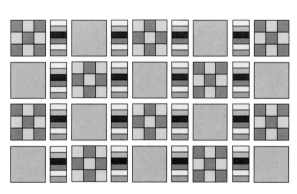

3-1/2"

Step 3

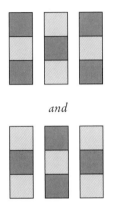

and

Step 2

Step 4

FIVE STRIPES

5″ block, straight set

Diana McClun and Laura Nownes; quilted by Anna Venti

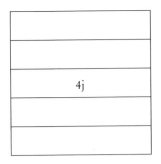

4j

5" block

	CRIB/WALL	TWIN	DOUBLE/QUEEN	KING
Finished size	*45" x 55"*	*75" x 95"*	*85" x 95"*	*105" x 95"*
Blocks set	9 x 11	15 x 19	17 x 19	21 x 19
Neutral blocks	32	94	104	128
Yellow blocks	17	49	57	71
Green blocks	16	48	52	64
Red blocks	16	50	58	68
Blue blocks	18	44	52	68

YARDAGE ▶

Neutrals: fabrics to total	1⅛	3	3⅜	4
Yellows: fabrics to total	⅞	2	2¼	2⅝
Greens: fabrics to total	⅞	2	2¼	2½
Reds: fabrics to total	1	2⅜	2½	3
Blues: fabrics to total	¾	1½	1¾	2¼
Backing	2⅞	4½	7½	8½
Binding	⅜	½	⅝	⅝

CUTTING ▶

TRADITIONAL:
Use template pattern 4j.

QUICK:

Neutrals: 1½"-wide strips	23	68	75	92
Yellows: 1½"-wide strips	18	44	50	61
Greens: 1½"-wide strips	17	44	47	56
Reds: 1½"-wide strips	22	54	57	69
Blues: 1½"-wide strips	13	32	38	49
Backing: lengths	2	2	3	3
See piecing diagram	B	A	C	C

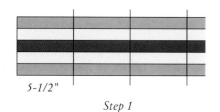

5-1/2"

Step 1

CONSTRUCTION

1. Sew several different combinations of strips together of each color into sets. Then cut the sets apart every 5½", as shown.

✂ *HELPFUL HINT*: Each set of strips will make seven blocks.

2. Lay out all the blocks, alternating the direction of the strips. Refer to the diagram for color placement. Then sew the blocks together in a straight set. Refer to Chapter 5 for specific instructions.

3. Sew strips together into sets for the pieced borders. If you cut the strips crosswise, it will first be necessary to join pieces together to make up the needed length for each side of your quilt. Be sure to allow enough extra fabric to miter the corners.

4. Sew the pieced borders to the quilt. Refer to Chapter 5 for specific instructions on mitered borders.

King   Twin   Crib/Wall   Twin   King

G		B	Y	R		G		B	Y	R	Y	B		G		R	Y		B		G
	B	Y	R		G		B	Y	R		R	Y	B		G		R	Y	B		
B	Y	R		G		B	Y	R		G		R	Y	B		G		R	Y	B	
Y	R		G		B	Y	R		G		G		R	Y	B		G		R	Y	
R		G		B	Y	R		G		B		G		R	Y	B		G		R	
	G		B	Y	R		G		B	Y	B		G		R	Y	B		G		
G		B	Y	R		G		B	Y	R	Y	B		G		R	Y	B		G	
	B	Y	R		G		B	Y	R		R	Y	B		G		R	Y	B		
B	Y	R		G		B	Y	R		G		R	Y	B		G		R	Y	B	
Y	R		G		B	Y	R		G	Y	G		R	Y	B		G		R	Y	
B	Y	R		G		B	Y	R		G		R	Y	B		G		R	Y	B	
	B	Y	R		G		B	Y	R		R	Y	B		G		R	Y	B		
G		B	Y	R		G		B	Y	R	Y	B		G		R	Y	B		G	
	G		B	Y	R		G		B	Y	B		G		R	Y	B		G		
R		G		B	Y	R		G		B		G		R	Y	B		G		R	
Y	R		G		B	Y	R		G		G		R	Y	B		G		R	Y	
B	Y	R		G		B	Y	R		G		R	Y	B		G		R	Y	B	
	B	Y	R		G		B	Y	R		R	Y	B		G		R	Y	B		
G		B	Y	R		G		B	Y	R	Y	B		G		R	Y	B		G	

D/Q   D/Q

Step 2

	= Neutral blocks
Y	= Yellow blocks
G	= Green blocks
R	= Red blocks
B	= Blue blocks

GARDEN MAZE

6″ blocks, straight set

Laura Nownes; quilted by JoAnn Manning

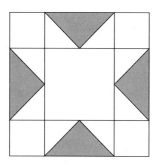

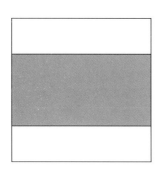

	CRIB/WALL	TWIN	DOUBLE/QUEEN	KING
Finished size	48" x 60"	72" x 84"	84" x 96"	108" x 96"
Blocks set	7 x 9	11 x 13	13 x 15	17 x 15
Block One	20	42	56	72
Block Two	31	71	97	127

YARDAGE ◀

Light-colored back-ground	2¼	3¾	5	6¼
Blue (includes binding)	2⅜	4¼	5½	7
Backing	3⅝	5	7½	8½

CUTTING ◀

TRADITIONAL:
Use template patterns 1b, 1d, 1f, 3e, 4e, 5d, and 6g.

QUICK:

	CRIB/WALL	TWIN	DOUBLE/QUEEN	KING
Light-colored background:				
2"-wide strips	12	24	32	42
Cut strips to 2" squares.				
3½"-wide strips	2	4	5	6
Cut strips to 3½" squares.				
2"-wide strips	18	32	45	55
Blue:				
2"-wide strips	6	8	11	11
3½"-wide strips	4	8	11	14
Cut strips to 2" x 3½" pieces.				
3½"-wide strips	1	1	1	1
Cut strips to 3½" squares.				
6½"-wide strips	2	5	7	10
Cut strips to 6½" squares.				
3½"-wide strips	6	12	17	22
Backing: lengths	2	2	3	3
See piecing diagram	B	A	D	C

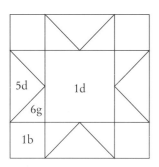

*Block One
6" Units*

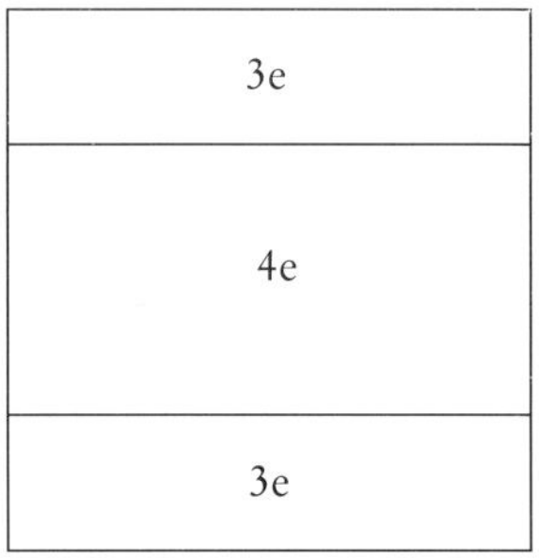

5d

1d

6g

1b

Block Two

3e

4e

3e

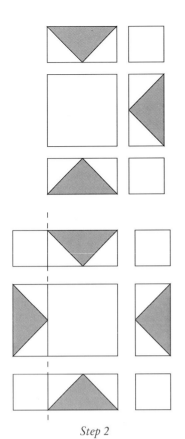

CONSTRUCTION

1. Make the required number of Block One blocks. Use the double half-square triangle technique with the 2″ squares of light background and 2″ x 3½″ blue pieces.

2. Block sew order: see diagram.

✀ *HELPFUL HINT*: Refer to the practice exercise for the double half-square triangle technique in Chapter 4 for help.

3. Make the required number of Block Two blocks. Join strips together to make sets. Then cut each set apart every 6½″, as shown.

✀ *HELPFUL HINT*: Each set will make six blocks.

4. Pieced border: Sew the remaining 2″-wide strips of blue and light-colored background together in sets. Cut every 6½″, as shown.

5. Lay out all the blocks, then sew them together in a straight set. Refer to Chapter 5 for specific instructions. Then attach the pieced border, as` shown.

Step 2

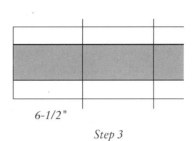

6-1/2″

Step 3

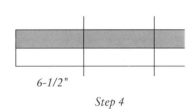

6-1/2″

Step 4

Step 5

BRASS RINGS

8¾" block, straight set with alternate blocks

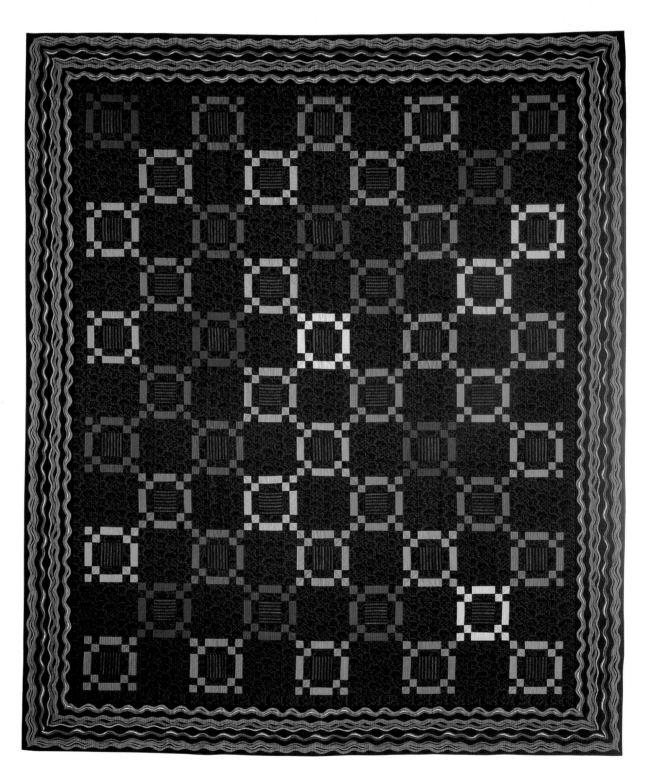

Diablo Valley Quilters to honor Alice Johns

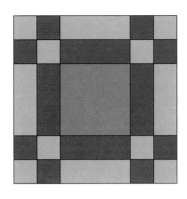

	CRIB/WALL	TWIN	DOUBLE/QUEEN	KING
Finished size	*53" x 53"*	*72" x 90"*	*90" x 90"*	*109" x 92"*
Blocks set	5 x 5	7 x 9	9 x 9	11 x 9
Pieced blocks	13	32	41	50
Units One and Two *each*	52	128	164	200
Alternate blocks	12	31	40	49

YARDAGE ▶

Black (includes binding)	2¼	4¼	5¼	6½
Bright solids: fabrics to total	¾	1⅜	1¾	2⅛
Stripe	⅜	⅝	¾	⅞
Outer border:				
Crosswise	⅝	1⅛	1¼	1⅝
or Lengthwise	1⅝	2⅝	2⅝	3⅛
Backing	3¼	5¼	8	8
Binding	⅜	⅝	⅝	¾

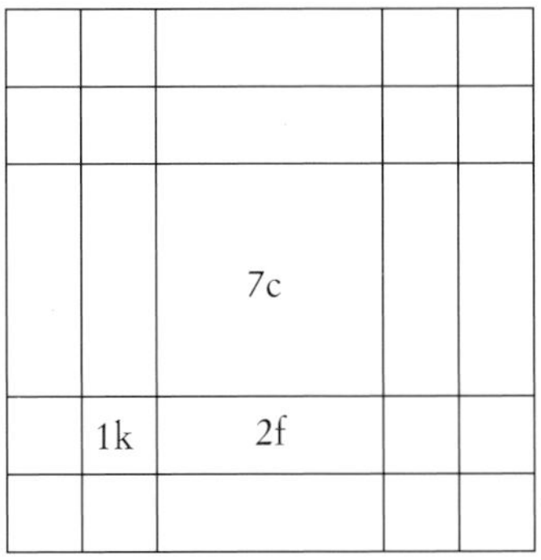

7c

1k   2f

8-3/4" block

CUTTING ▶

If you are cutting the inner border lengthwise, cut the strips *before* cutting the other shapes from the black fabric.

TRADITIONAL:
Use template patterns 1k, 2f, and 7c. There is no template pattern for the alternate block. You can make a 9¼" square from template plastic if you so desire.

QUICK:
Black: Cut inner border first then use remaining width to cut alternate blocks.

9¼"-wide strips	4	11	12	15
Cut strips to 9¼" squares.				
1¾"-wide strips	11	26	33	40
Bright solids:				
1¾"-wide strips	11	26	33	40
Stripe: 4¼"-wide strips	2	4	5	6
Cut strips to 4¼" squares.				

BORDERS AND BACKING:

Black inner border:				
2"-wide strips:				
Crosswise	6	8	9	10
or Lengthwise	4	4	4	4
Outer border: width	3½"	4½"	4½"	5½"
Crosswise	5	8	9	10
or Lengthwise	4	4	4	4
Backing: lengths	2	2	3	3
See piecing diagram	A	A	C	C

Unit One   Unit Two

CONSTRUCTION

1. Sew black and bright solid strips together in pairs. ✄ *HELPFUL HINT:* Each pieced block requires a 31″ strip *each* of black and bright solid. Three sets will make four pieced blocks.

2. To make Unit One, cut the sets apart every 1¾″, making eight cuts, as shown. Then make four 4¼″ cuts to make Unit Two, as shown.

3. Unit One, sew order: see diagram.

4. Block sew order: see diagram.

5. Lay out all the pieced blocks and alternate blocks.

6. Sew the blocks together in a straight set. Refer to Chapter 5 for specific instructions.

7. Attach inner and outer borders, mitering corners, as shown.

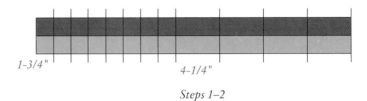

1-3/4″   4-1/4″

Steps 1–2

Unit One

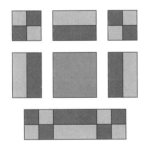

Step 3

Step 4

Step 7

NINE-PATCH
3¾″ block, diagonal set with alternate blocks

Collection of Diana McClun, c. 1930

▼

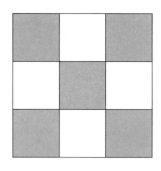

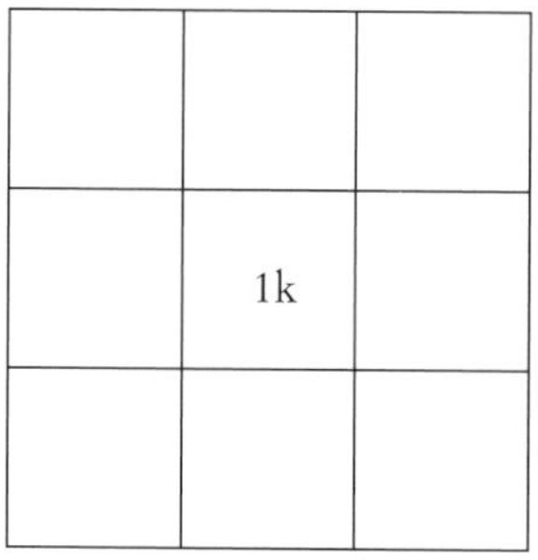

3-3/4" block

	CRIB/WALL	TWIN	DOUBLE/QUEEN	KING
Finished size	37" x 58"	68" x 89"	89" x 89"	100" x 100"
Blocks set	6 x 10	12 x 16	16 x 16	18 x 18
Pieced blocks	75	240	320	405
Alternate blocks	30	117	161	208

YARDAGE ◀

	CRIB/WALL	TWIN	DOUBLE/QUEEN	KING
Light-colored background	1	2¼	2⅞	3½
Pieced blocks and pieced border: fabrics to total	1⅝	4¾	6¼	8
Inner border (top and bottom) and binding:				
Crosswise	⅝	¾	1	1
or Lengthwise	1⅛	2	2½	2⅞
Backing	1¾	5⅜	8	8¾

CUTTING ◀

TRADITIONAL:
Use template patterns 1k, 5b, 6b, and 7c.

QUICK:

	CRIB/WALL	TWIN	DOUBLE/QUEEN	KING
Light-colored background:				
4¼"-wide strips	4	13	18	24
Cut strips to 4¼" squares.				
6¾"-wide strips	2	3	3	3
Cut strips to 6¾" squares. Then cut the squares into quarters diagonally.				
3¾" squares	2	2	2	2
Cut each square in half diagonally.				
Pieced blocks and pieced border:				
1¾"-wide strips	31	95	126	159
BORDER AND BACKING:				
Border:				
1¾"-wide strips				
Crosswise	2	4	5	5
or Lengthwise	2	2	2	2
Backing: lengths	1	2	3	3
See piecing diagram	—	A	C	C

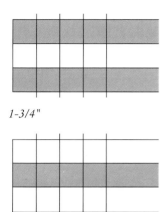

1-3/4"

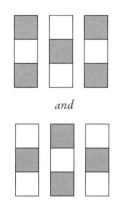

1-3/4"

Step 1

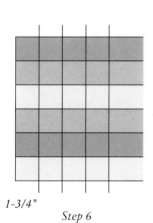

and

Step 2

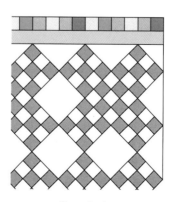

1-3/4"   *Step 6*

1. Make the required number of nine-patch blocks: sew several different combinations of strips. Then cut the sets apart every 1¾", as shown.

✂ *HELPFUL HINT*: Each pair of sets will make sixteen nine-patch blocks.

2. Sew order: see diagrams.

3. Lay out the nine-patch blocks, alternate blocks, and side and corner triangles, as shown.

4. Sew all the blocks together in a diagonal set. Refer to Chapter 5 for spe-cific instructions. Side and corner triangles are cut slightly too big. Straighten the edges and remove the excess to within ⅜" of the corners of the blocks.

5. Sew an inner border strip to the top and bottom edges of the quilt only.

6. To make the pieced border: sew remaining strips together in sets. Then cut the sets apart every 1¾", as shown. Join enough pieced strips together for the top and bottom edges of the quilt. Attach them to complete the quilt top.

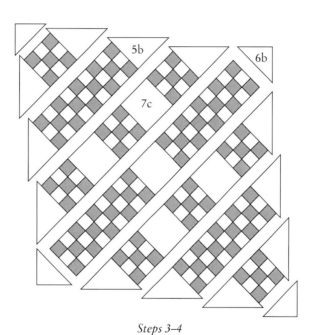

Steps 3–4

Steps 5–6

TREASURED HEARTS

6" block, straight set

Tricia Thomas and friends for Pauline Stone Mead; quilted by Anna Venti

	CRIB/WALL	TWIN	DOUBLE/QUEEN	KING
Finished size	*40" x 56"*	*72" x 88"*	*88" x 96"*	*104" x 96"*
Blocks set	4 x 6	8 x 10	10 x 11	12 x 11
Total blocks	24	80	110	132

YARDAGE

Background	⅞	2¾	3⅝	4¼
Hearts	½	1½	2⅛	2⅜
Sashing and border*	2	1¾	3	3¼
Backing	2½	5¼	7¾	8½
Binding	⅜	½	⅝	⅝

*Extra length is given on border fabric to allow for centering designs.

CUTTING

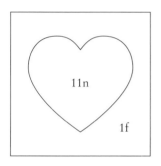

6" block

TRADITIONAL:
Use template patterns 1f and 11n.

QUICK:				
6½"-wide strips	4	14	20	22
Cut strips to 6½" squares.				
Hearts: use (11n)	24	80	120	132

SASHING, BORDER, AND BACKING:				
Sashing: width*	2½"	2½"	2½"	2½"
Border: width*	5½"	5½"	5½"	5½"
Backing: lengths	2	2	3	3
See piecing diagram	B	A	D	C

*Widths may vary with the design of your border-printed fabric.

CONSTRUCTION

1. Appliqué the hearts to the background fabric, using one of the appliqué techniques described in Chapter 4.

2. Lay out all the blocks. Sew them together in a straight set with sashing strips. Refer to Chapter 5 for specific instructions.

3. Attach the border strips. Refer to Chapter 5 for help in attaching border-printed fabrics.

Steps 2–3

VESTIBULE

5" block, straight set with pieced sashing units and posts

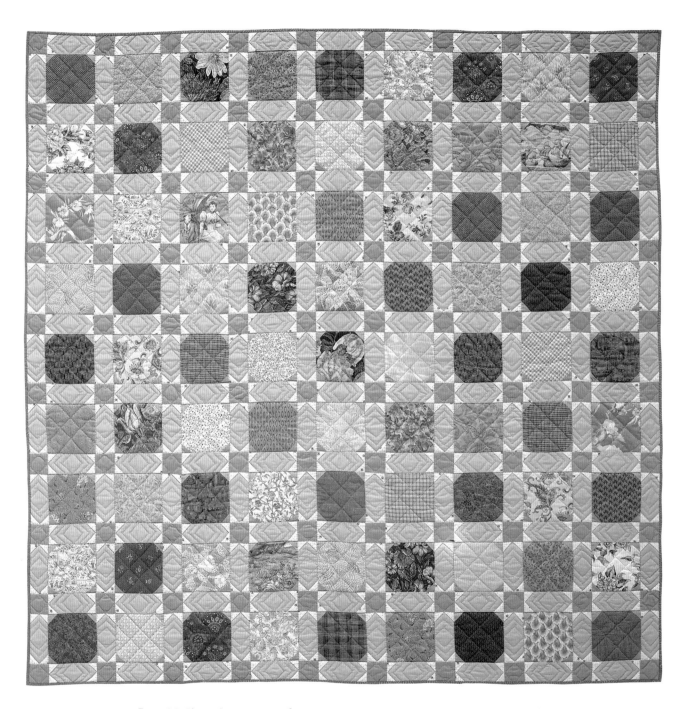

Diana McClun and Laura Nownes for Laura's parents, Jane and Tom Smith; quilted by Anna Venti

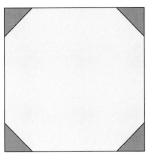

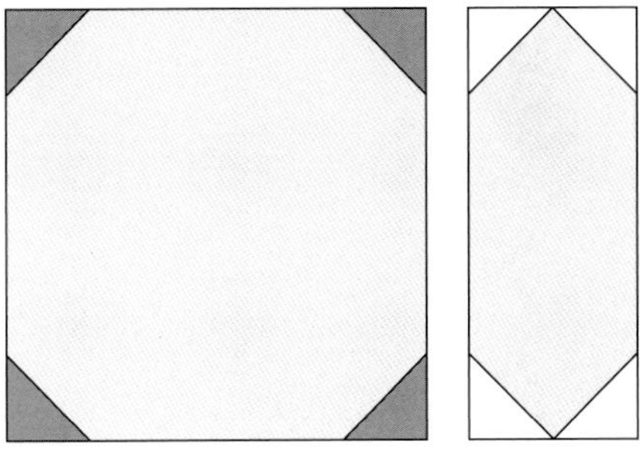

	CRIB/WALL	TWIN	DOUBLE/QUEEN	KING
Finished size	*44″ x 58″*	*72″ x 86″*	*86″ x 93″*	*100″ x 100″*
Blocks set	6 x 8	10 x 12	12 x 13	14 x 14
Pieced blocks	48	120	156	196
Sashing units	114	266	338	420

YARDAGE ▶

	CRIB/WALL	TWIN	DOUBLE/QUEEN	KING
Pieced blocks:				
Centers: fabrics to total	1¼	2⅞	3⅝	4⅜
Corners	⅜	⅞	1⅛	1¼
Sashing units:				
Background	1⅜	2⅝	3½	4¼
Corners	1	1¾	2¼	2⅝
Posts	⅜	¾	1	1¼
Backing	2¾	4⅜	5½	8¾
Binding	⅜	½	½	⅝

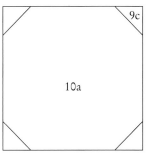

5" block

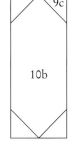

Sashing unit

1c

Post

CUTTING ▶

TRADITIONAL:
Use template patterns 1c, 9c, 10a, and 10b.

QUICK:

	CRIB/WALL	TWIN	DOUBLE/QUEEN	KING
Pieced blocks:				
Centers, 5½″ squares	48	120	156	196
Corners, 1½″-wide strips	7	18	23	28
Cut strips to 1½″ squares.				
Sashing units:				
Background: 5½″-wide strips	8	17	22	27
Cut strips to 2½″ x 5½″ pieces.				
Corners: 1½″-wide strips	17	38	49	60
Cut strips to 1½″ squares.				
Posts: 2½″-wide strips	4	9	12	15
Cut strips to 2½″ squares.				
Backing: lengths	2	2	2	3
See piecing diagram	B	B	A	C

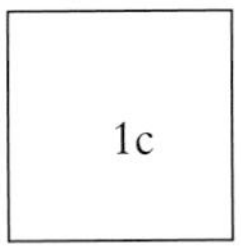

33
▼

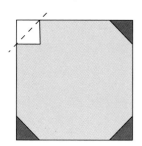

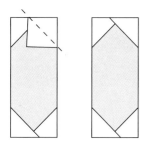

Step 1

CONSTRUCTION

1. Make the required number of pieced blocks. Use the double half-square triangle technique to attach the corners to the center square, as shown.

2. Make the required number of sashing units. Use the double half-square triangle technique to attach the corners, as shown.

3. Lay out all the pieced blocks, alternating with sashing units, as shown. Then sew all the units together in a straight set. Refer to Chapter 5 for specific instructions.

Step 2

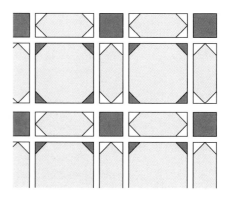

Step 3

BASKET

5" block, diagonal set with sashing and posts

Rosalee Sanders

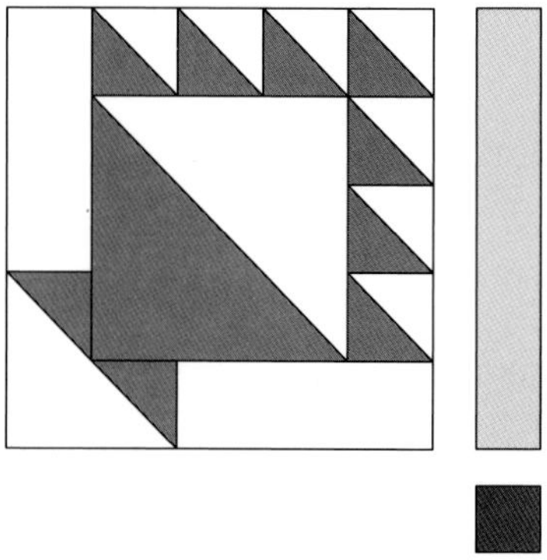

	CRIB/WALL	TWIN	DOUBLE/QUEEN	KING
Finished size	*44″ x 60″*	*68″ x 93″*	*85″ x 93″*	*101″ x 101″*
Blocks set	4 x 6	7 x 10	9 x 10	11 x 11
Total blocks	39	124	162	221
Side triangles	16	30	34	40

YARDAGE

Pieced blocks: fabrics to total	2	5½	7	9¼
Sashing	⅝	1½	1¾	2½
Posts	⅛	¼	¼	⅜
Side and corner triangles, outer border and binding	1⅞	2¾	2¾	3
Inner border:				
Crosswise	⅜	½	½	⅝
or Lengthwise	1½	2½	2½	2⅝
Backing	4	5½	5½	9

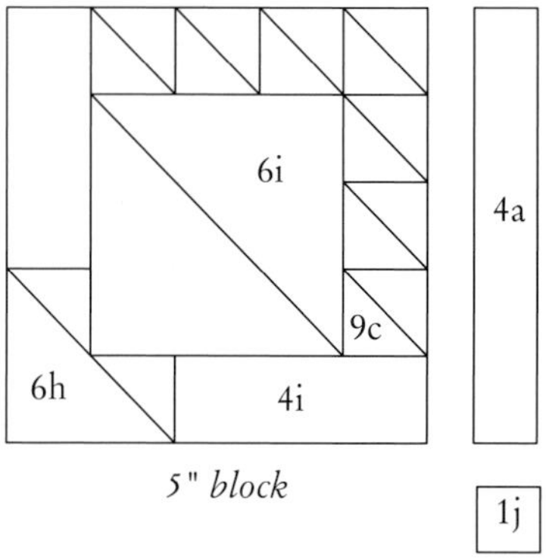

5" block

CUTTING

TRADITIONAL:

Use template patterns 1j, 4a, 4i, 6h, 6i, and 9c.

QUICK:

Template patterns are not required for quick-cutting. They are used only to identify the shapes.

Pieced blocks:				
(4i), 3½″-wide strips	3	9	12	16
Cut strips to 1½″ x 3½″ pieces.				
(6h), 2⅞″-wide strips	2	5	6	8
Cut strips to 2⅞″ squares. Then cut the squares in half diagonally.				
(6i), 3⅞″-wide strips	4	13	17	23
Cut strips to 3⅞″ squares. Then cut the squares in half diagonally.				
(9c), 1⅞″-wide strips	15	48	62	85
Cut strips to 1⅞″ squares. Then cut the squares in half diagonally.				
Sashing:				
5½″-wide strips	3	9	11	15
Posts:				
1¼″-wide strips	2	5	7	8
Cut strips to 1¼″ squares.				

	CRIB/WALL	TWIN	DOUBLE/QUEEN	KING
ALSO NEEDED:				
Outer border:				
4½″-wide strips	4	4	4	4
Side triangles:				
10½″ squares	4	8	9	10
Cut the squares into quarters diagonally.				
Corner triangles:				
6″ squares	2	2	2	2
Cut the squares in half diagonally.				
Inner border:				
1¾″-wide strips:				
Crosswise	5	8	9	10
or Lengthwise	4	4	4	4
Backing: lengths	2	2	2	3
See piecing diagram	B	A	A	C

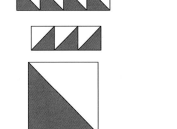

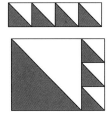

Step 2

CONSTRUCTION

1. Make half-square triangle units. Seven are needed for each block. Check for accuracy: each unit should measure 1½″.

2. Unit construction: see diagrams.

3. Block sew order: see diagrams.

4. Lay out all the pieced blocks, side and corner triangles. Join them with sashing and posts in a diagonal set. Refer to Chapter 5 for specific instructions.

5. Join the inner and outer border strips in pairs. Then attach them to the quilt top, mitering the corners.

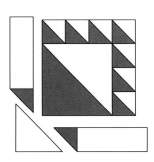

Step 3

Steps 4–5

SAWTOOTH

10″ block, straight set

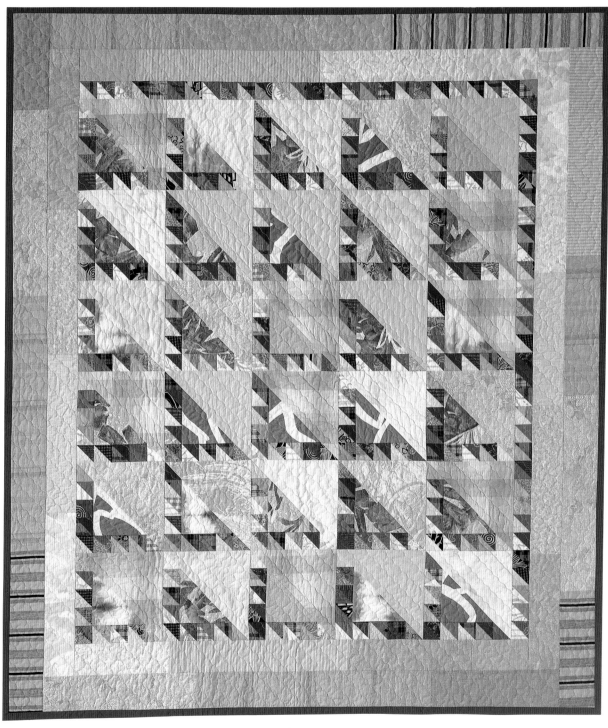

Rebecca Rohrkaste

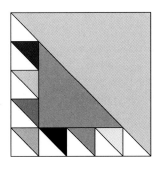

	CRIB/WALL	TWIN	DOUBLE/QUEEN	KING
Finished size	*50" x 60"*	*70" x 90"*	*90" x 90"*	*100" x 100"*
Blocks set	3 x 4	5 x 7	7 x 7	8 x 8
Total blocks	12	35	49	64

YARDAGE ◀

Pieced blocks and border (two sides only): fabrics to total	1¾	4½	6½	8
Borders: fabrics to total	1⅜	2	2¼	2½
Backing	3	5¼	7¾	8½
Binding (⅞"-wide)	1	1⅛	1¼	1¼

CUTTING ◀

TRADITIONAL:

Use template patterns 6e and 6h. There is no template patterns for the large triangle. You can make a 10⅞" triangle from template plastic if you so desire.

QUICK:

2⅞"-wide strips	7	23	32	41
Cut strips to 2⅞" squares. Then cut the squares in half diagonally.				
6⅞"-wide strips	1	3	5	6
Cut strips to 6⅞" squares. Then cut the squares in half diagonally.				
10⅞" squares	6	18	25	32
Cut the squares in half diagonally.				

BORDERS AND BACKING:

Borders: Various lengths are used and sewn together to measure the needed lengths.

Inner border strips: width	4"	4"	4"	4"
Outer border strips: width	4¾"	4¾"	4¾"	4¾"
Backing: lengths	2	2	3	3
See piecing diagram	B	A	C	C

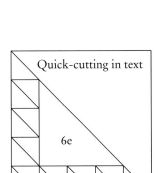

Quick-cutting in text

6e

6h

10" block

and

Step 2

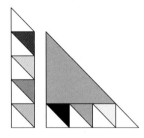

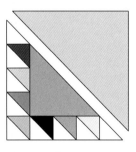

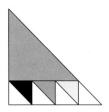

Step 3

CONSTRUCTION

1. Make seven half-square triangle units for each pieced block. Check for accuracy: each unit should measure 2½".

2. Unit construction: see diagrams.

3. Block sew order: see diagrams.

4. Lay out all the blocks. Sew them together in a straight set. Refer to Chapter 5 for specific instructions.

5. Half-square triangle units are sewn in strips and added to two adjoining sides to complete the sawtooth design around the edge.

6. Sew pieces of border strips together to measure the needed length for each side of the quilt. Then attach them to the quilt. Refer to Chapter 5 for help.

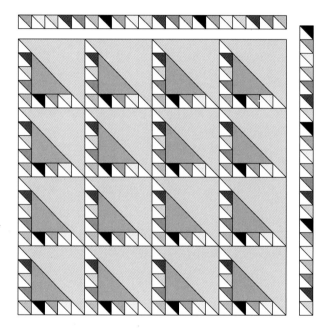

Steps 4–5

BAR QUILT
Vertical set with sashing strips

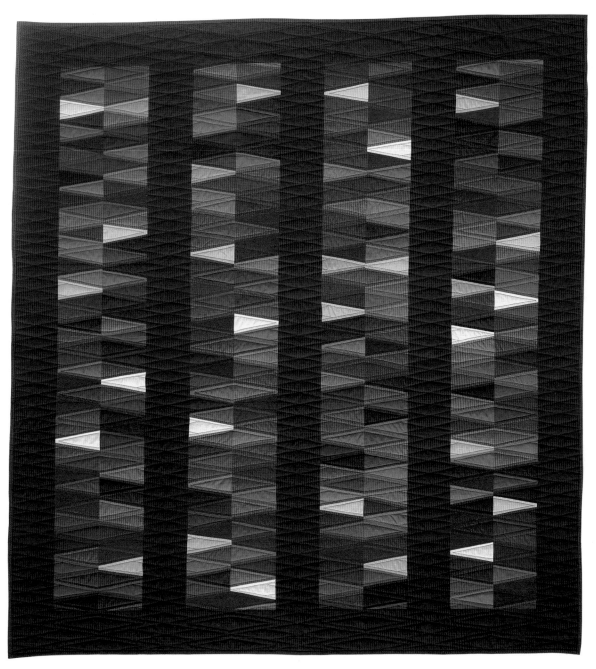

Mabry Benson

	TWIN	DOUBLE/QUEEN	KING
Finished size	*68″ x 89″*	*84″ x 89″*	*100″ x 102″*
Vertical sets	4	5	6
Shapes per single row	59	59	69
Total shapes	472	590	828

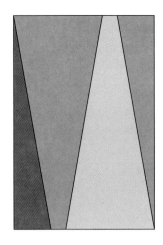

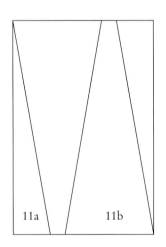

YARDAGE

SASHING AND BORDER:			
Crosswise	2¼	2⅝	3½
or Lengthwise	2¼	4¾	5½
Bright solids; fabrics to total	3¾	4¾	6¾
Backing	5½	7½	9
Binding	½	½	⅝

CUTTING

TRADITIONAL:

Use template patterns 11a and 11b. ☞ *WARNING*: Remember to reverse the cutting direction for one-half of the (11a) shapes.

QUICK:

5⅝″-wide strips	14	18	21

Use with (11a and 11b) to mark angles for cutting. One (11a) is needed for the end of each single row. Reverse the shape on opposite ends.

SASHING AND BORDER: 5¾″-wide strips:			
Crosswise	13	16	21
or Lengthwise	7	8	9
Backing: lengths	2	2	3
See piecing diagram	A	A	C

CONSTRUCTION

1. Make single rows: unit construction, see diagrams. Sew half shapes (11a) at each end.

2. Join single rows to make vertical sets, as shown.

3. Join the side borders, vertical sets, and sashing strips. Refer to the photo.

4. Attach the top and bottom borders to complete the quilt top.

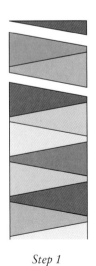

Step 1

Step 2

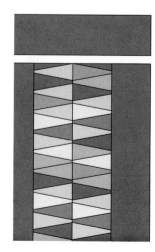

Steps 3–4

BOW TIE

6" and 12" blocks, straight set

Diana McClun and Laura Nownes; quilted by JoAnn Manning

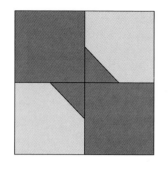

	CRIB/WALL	TWIN	DOUBLE/QUEEN	KING
Finished size	*45" x 57"*	*69" x 92"*	*92" x 92"*	*104" x 92"*
Blocks set	3 x 4	5 x 7	7 x 7	8 x 7
6" blocks	12	28	36	44
12" blocks	9	28	40	45

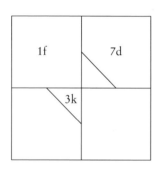

YARDAGE

	CRIB/WALL	TWIN	DOUBLE/QUEEN	KING
Background: fabrics to total	1¼	3⅛	4	4¼
Bow Ties: fabrics to total	1½	3⅝	4⅞	5⅜
Light border background	⅞	1⅛	1¼	1⅜
Backing	2⅞	5½	8	8
Binding	⅜	½	⅝	⅝

CUTTING

TRADITIONAL:
Use template patterns 1d, 1f, 3k, 3m, 5c, 6b, 6g, 7b, and 7d.

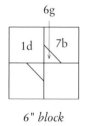

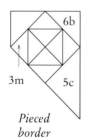

12" block

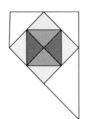

6g

1d 7b

6" block

6b
3m 5c

Pieced
border

QUICK:

	CRIB/WALL	TWIN	DOUBLE/QUEEN	KING
6" blocks:				
Background fabrics:				
3½"-wide strips	2	5	6	8
Cut strips to 3½" squares.				
Bow Tie fabrics:				
2"-wide strips	1	1	1	1
Cut strips to 2" squares.				
3½"-wide strips	2	5	6	8
Cut strips to 3½" squares.				
12" blocks:				
Background fabrics:				
6½"-wide strips	3	10	11	15
Cut strips to 6½" squares.				
Bow Tie fabrics:				
3⅛"-wide strips	2	5	6	8
Cut strips to 3⅛" squares.				
6½"-wide strips	3	10	11	15
Cut strips to 6½" squares.				
Pieced border:				
Background and Bow Tie fabrics:				
2¾"-wide strips, *each*	5	8	8	9
Cut strips to 2¾" squares. Then cut the squares in half diagonally.				
Light background:				
6¾"-wide strips	4	6	6	7
Cut strips to 6¾" squares. Then cut the squares into quarters diagonally (side triangles).				

	CRIB/WALL	TWIN	DOUBLE/QUEEN	KING
3¾″ squares	2	2	2	2
Cut square in half diagonally (corner triangle).				
Backing: lengths	2	2	3	3
See piecing diagram	B	A	C	C

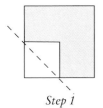

Step 1

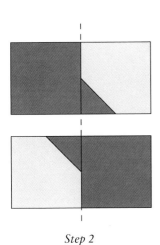

Step 2

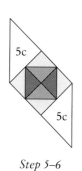

Step 5–6

CONSTRUCTION

1. Make the required number of 6″ and 12″ blocks. Unit construction: see diagram. Use the double half-square triangle technique when attaching the small squares of bow tie fabric to the large squares of background fabric. Save the bonus half-square triangle units to use in the pieced border.

2. Block sew order: see diagram.

3. Lay out all the blocks. Then sew them together in a straight set. Refer to Chapter 5 for specific instructions.

4. Trim the bonus half-square triangle units to measure 2″. Make additional half-square triangle units for the pieced border.

5. Unit construction for pieced border: see diagram.

6. Sew enough units together for each side of the quilt top. Side triangles are cut a little too big. Straighten the edges and remove the excess to within ⅜″ of the corners of the pieced units. Then sew the pieced border to the quilt top.

☞ *WARNING*: Since there are variations in cutting and sewing, opposite corners may differ, similar to our sample. Refer to the diagram for help. Also, you may need to add an adjustment strip before adding the pieced border. See Chapter 5 for specific instructions.

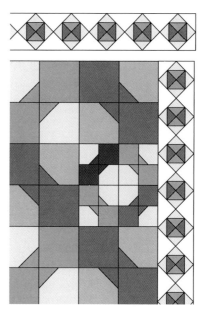

Step 6

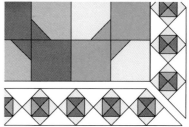

PIECED BUTTERCUP

6″ block, straight set

An original pattern by Mary Ellen Hopkins

Bernice McCoy Stone

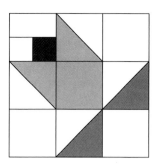

	CRIB/WALL	TWIN	DOUBLE/QUEEN	KING
Finished size	*48″ x 58″*	*70″ x 88″*	*88″ x 94″*	*100″ x 94″*
Blocks set	7 x 9	11 x 14	14 x 15	16 x 15
Total blocks	63	154	210	240

YARDAGE ◀

	CRIB/WALL	TWIN	DOUBLE/QUEEN	KING
Light-colored back-ground	2¾	5½	7¼	8¼
Red (includes binding)	1½	1⅞	2¼	2⅜
Flowers: fabrics to total	⅞	1¾	2⅜	2¾
Leaves	½	1	1⅜	1⅝
Backing	3	5¼	7¾	8¼

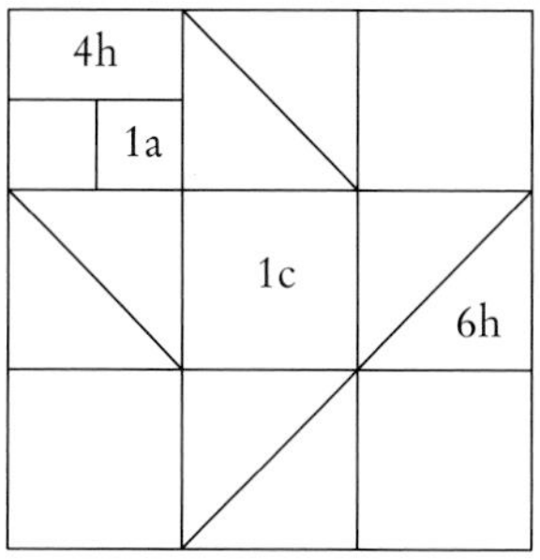

CUTTING ◀

TRADITIONAL:
Use template patterns 1a, 1c, 4h, 6h, and 9c.

QUICK:

	CRIB/WALL	TWIN	DOUBLE/QUEEN	KING
Light-colored background:				
1½″-wide strips	7	16	22	24
2½″-wide strips	12	29	40	45
Cut strips to 2½″ squares.				
2⅞″-wide strips	9	22	30	35
Cut strips to 2⅞″ squares. Then cut the squares in half diagonally.				
1⅞″-wide strips★	11	16	18	19
Cut strips to 1⅞″ squares. Then cut the squares in half diagonally.				
Red:				
1½″-wide strips	3	6	8	9
1⅞″-wide strips★	11	16	18	19
Cut strips to 1⅞″ squares. Then cut the squares in half diagonally.				
Flowers:				
2½″-wide strips	4	10	14	16
Cut strips to 2½″ squares.				
2⅞″-wide strips	5	11	15	18
Cut strips to 2⅞″ squares. Then cut the squares in half diagonally.				
Leaves:				
2⅞″-wide strips	5	11	15	18

6″ block

Sawtooth border

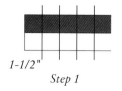

1-1/2"

Step 1

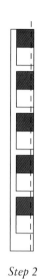

Step 2

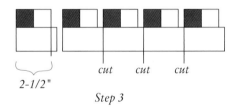

2-1/2"

Step 3

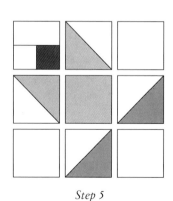

Step 5

Cut strips to 2⅞" squares.
  Then cut the squares in
  half diagonally.

	CRIB/WALL	TWIN	DOUBLE/QUEEN	KING
Backing: lengths	2	2	3	3
See piecing diagram	B	A	D	C

*Layer fabrics before cutting (sawtooth border).

CONSTRUCTION

1. Sew 1½"-wide red and light-colored background strips together. Then cut them apart every 1½", as shown.
✂ *HELPFUL HINT*: Cut one unit for each block. Each set will make 28 units.

2. Sew the units made in Step 1 to 1½"-wide strips of light background, as shown.

3. Press toward the solid strip. Then cut the units apart, as shown. Trim the excess fabric and straighten the edges.

4. Make half-square triangle units.

Check for accuracy: each unit should measure 2½".

5. Block sew order: see diagram.

6. Lay out all the blocks. Sew them together in a straight set. Refer to Chapter 5 for specific instructions.

7. Make the half-square triangles for the pieced border. Check for accuracy: each unit should measure 1½". Lay them out and then sew them together to make a double sawtooth border.

Steps 6–7

▼

JEWEL BOX

6″ block, straight set with sashing and posts

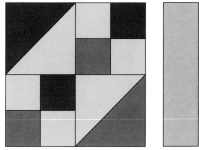

	CRIB/WALL	TWIN	DOUBLE/QUEEN	KING
Finished size	*45″ x 59″*	*74″ x 89″*	*89″ x 96″*	*104″ x 96″*
Blocks set	6 x 8	10 x 12	12 x 13	14 x 13
Total blocks	48	120	156	182

YARDAGE

Lights (stripes and shirtings): fabrics to total	2⅛	4¾	6¼	7½
Darks (plaids): fabrics to total	1⅜	3	4⅛	4¾
Backing	3	5½	8	8½
Binding (pieced plaids)	⅜	½	⅝	⅝

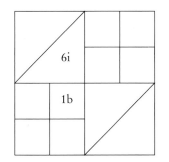

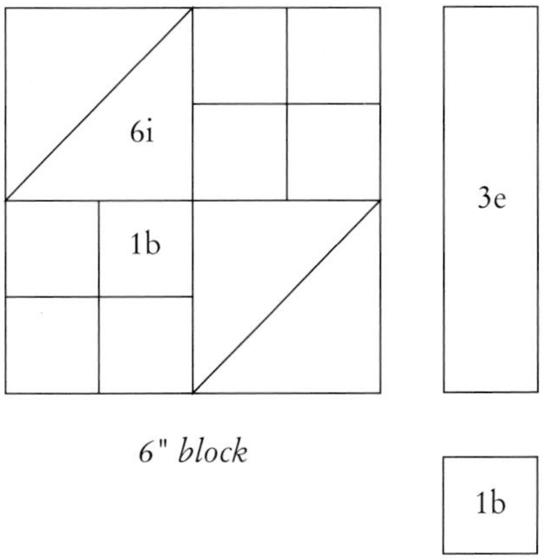

6″ block

CUTTING

TRADITIONAL:
Use template patterns 1b, 3e, and 6i.

QUICK:

Lights:				
2″-wide strips	10	23	30	35
3⅞″-wide strips	5	12	16	19
Cut strips to 3⅞″ squares. Then cut the squares in half diagonally.				
2″-wide strips (for sashing)	14	37	48	57
Cut strips to 2″ x 6½″ pieces.				
Darks:				
2″-wide strips (for posts)	2	5	7	8
Cut strips to 2″ squares.				
3⅞″-wide strips	5	12	16	19
Cut strips to 3⅞″ squares. Then cut the squares in half diagonally.				
2″-wide strips	10	23	30	35
Backing: lengths	2	2	3	3
See piecing diagram	B	A	D	C

Sandy Klop and friends; quilted by Sandy Klop

2"

Step 1

Step 2

Step 4

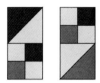

Step 5

CONSTRUCTION

1. Sew a variety of combinations of light and dark strips in pairs, as shown. Then cut the sets apart every 2".

✂ *HELPFUL HINT*: You can layer the sets for cutting if the seams are opposing on alternate sets.

2. Unit construction: see diagram.

3. Sew light and dark triangles together in pairs to make half-square triangle units. Check for accuracy: each unit should measure 3½".

4. Unit construction: see diagram.

5. Block sew order: see diagram.

6. Lay out all the blocks, alternating direction and separating with sashing and posts, as shown. Then sew all the pieces together in a straight set. Refer to Chapter 5 for specific instructions.

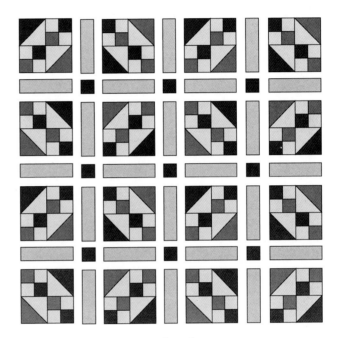

Step 6

ALBUM PATCH

12″ block, straight set with sashing

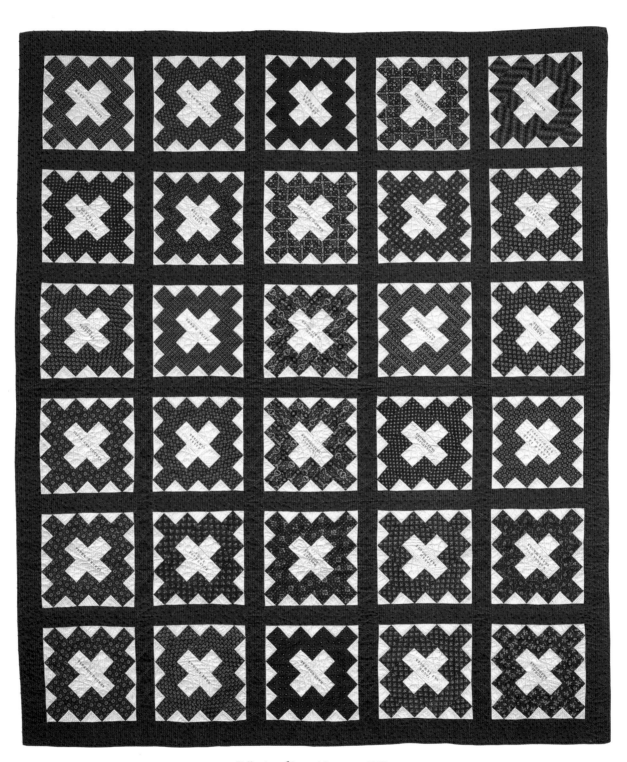

Collection of Laura Nownes, c. 1851

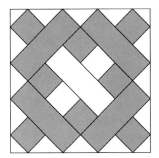

	CRIB/WALL	TWIN	DOUBLE/QUEEN	KING
Finished size	*47" x 61"*	*75" x 90"*	*89" x 90"*	*104" x 104"*
Blocks set	3 x 4	5 x 6	6 x 6	7 x 7
Total blocks	12	30	36	49

YARDAGE ▶

Light-colored background	1¼	2½	3⅛	4¼
Reds (pieced blocks)	1¼	2⅞	3¼	4⅝
Red (sashing, border, and binding)	1¾	2⅝	2⅝	3
Backing	2⅞	5⅜	8	9

CUTTING ▶

TRADITIONAL:
Use template patterns 1g, 3j, 5h, and 9d.

QUICK:

Light-colored background:				
2⅝"-wide strips	2	4	5	7
6⅞"-wide strips	1	2	3	4
Cut strips to 2⅝" x 6⅞" pieces.				
4½"-wide strips	4	10	12	17
Cut strips to 4½" squares. Then cut squares into quarters diagonally.				
2⅝"-wide strips	2	4	5	6
Cut strips to 2⅝" squares. Then cut the squares in half diagonally.				
Reds (pieced blocks):				
2⅝"-wide strips	6	15	18	25
6⅞"-wide strips	3	8	9	13
Cut strips to 2⅝" x 6⅞" pieces.				
SASHING, BORDER, AND BACKING:				
Sashing: width	2¾"	2¾"	2¾"	2¾"
Border: width	3½"	3½"	3½"	3½"
Backing: lengths	2	2	3	3
See piecing diagram	B	A	C	C

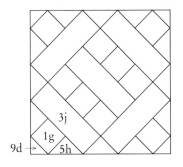

12" block

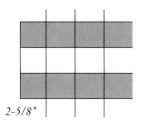

2-5/8"

Step 1

Make one for each block.

Make two for each block.

Make two for each block.

Step 3

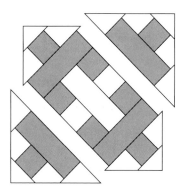

Step 4

CONSTRUCTION

The signatures on the sample quilt were done in cross stitch. You could also use a fine-line permanent pen.

1. Sew red and light-colored background strips together in sets. Then cut them apart every 2⅝", as shown. Make enough sets for the total blocks needed. ✂ *HELPFUL HINT*: Each set makes eight blocks.

2. Cut the remaining 2⅝"-wide red strips to 2⅝" squares.

3. Unit construction: see diagrams.

4. Block construction: see diagram. Side and corner triangles are cut too large. Trim the blocks to measure 12½" square.

5. Lay out all the blocks. Sew the pieced blocks and sashing strips in a straight set. Refer to Chapter 5 for specific instructions.

6. Attach the border to complete the quilt top.

Step 6

FREDDY'S HOUSE

8" block, straight set

An original pattern by Freddy Moran

Freddy Moran; quilted by Kathy Sandbach

	CRIB/WALL	TWIN	DOUBLE/QUEEN	KING
Finished size	*42" x 58"*	*74" x 90"*	*90" x 90"*	*106" x 98"*
Blocks set	4 x 6	8 x 10	10 x 10	12 x 11
Total blocks	24	80	100	132

YARDAGE

Houses: fabrics to total	1½	4⅛	5¼	7
Sashing (black and white prints): fabrics to total	¾	3⅜	4½	6
Inner border:				
Crosswise	¼	⅜	⅜	½
or Lengthwise	1½	2¼	2¼	2¾
Outer border:				
Crosswise	¾	1⅛	1¼	1⅜
or Lengthwise	1¾	2⅝	2⅝	3
Backing	2⅝	5⅜	8	8½
Binding	⅜	½	⅝	¾

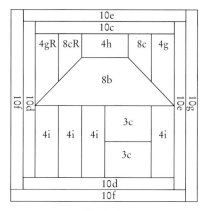

8" block

CUTTING

TRADITIONAL:
Use template patterns 3c, 4g, 4h, 4i, 8b, 8c, 10c, 10d, 10e, 10f, and 10g.
☞ *WARNING*: Remember to reverse the direction for one-half of the chimney (8c) and sky (4g) shapes. ✂ *HELPFUL HINT*: Remember to transfer the dots from (8b and 8c) onto the fabric shapes.

QUICK:
To achieve a scrap look similar to the sample quilt, make each block different. Individual shape sizes and amounts are given.

House front:				
1½" x 3½" pieces	72	240	300	396
2" x 2½" pieces	24	80	100	132
Doors: 1½" x 3½" pieces	24	80	100	132
Windows: 2" x 2½" pieces	24	80	100	132
Sky:				
1½" x 2½" pieces	24	80	100	132
1½" x 3⅞" pieces	48	160	200	264
Chimneys: 1½" x 2⅞" pieces	48	160	200	264
Roofs: use (8b)	24	80	100	132

SASHING, BORDERS, AND BACKING:
Sashing: Cut all of the sashing fabrics into 1"-wide strips.

Inner border: 1½"-wide strips:				
Crosswise	6	7	8	9
or Lengthwise	4	4	4	4
Outer border: 4½"-wide strips:				
Crosswise	6	8	9	11
or Lengthwise	4	4	4	4
Backing: lengths	2	2	3	3
See piecing diagram	B	A	C	C

CONSTRUCTION

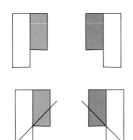

Step 1

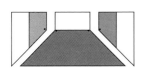

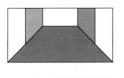

Step 2–3

Step 4

Step 5

1. Unit construction: see diagram.

✄ *HELPFUL HINT*: Finger press a center-point fold along the bottom edge of the sky piece and the top edge of the roof. Match the center points and secure them with a pin. With the sky shape on top, sew the two shapes together, beginning and ending ¼″ from the ends, as indicated by the dots in the diagram.

2. If using quick-cutting methods, simply join the sky and chimney strips, as shown.

3. Lay the 45° angle on your wide plastic ruler over the strips, making certain the straight edge of the ruler is in line with the edge of one strip. Then use the rotary cutter to remove the excess, as shown.

4. Sew the sky/chimney unit to the sky/roof unit. Do not stitch into the seam allowance. Stop ¼″ from the end, as indicated by the dots in the diagram.

5. Block sew order: see diagram.

6. Working counterclockwise, sew the sashing strips to the blocks, trimming the excess, as shown.

7. Lay out all of the blocks. Then sew them together in a straight set. Refer to Chapter 5 for specific instructions.

8. Attach the inner and then outer borders to complete the quilt top.

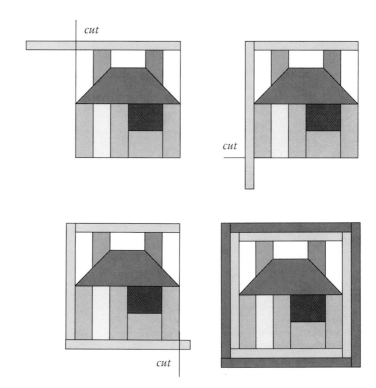

Step 6

SAILBOAT

12″ block, straight set

Diana McClun and friends for grandson Joe Thomas; quilted by Anna Venti

▼

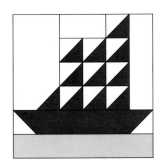

Block One

Block Two

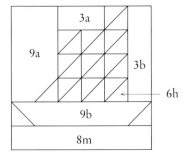

12" block

	CRIB/WALL	TWIN	DOUBLE/QUEEN	KING
Finished size	*56" x 56"*	*68" x 92"*	*92" x 92"*	*104" x 92"*
Blocks set	3 x 3	4 x 6	6 x 6	7 x 6
Block One	4	12	18	21
Block Two	5	12	18	21

YARDAGE ▶

Light-colored back-ground	2¼	3¼	4½	5
Navy	2¼	3¼	4½	5
Border fabric*:				
Crosswise	1⅛	1½	1⅝	2
or Lengthwise	1⅝	2⅝	2⅝	3
Backing	3½	5½	8	8
Binding	⅜	½	⅝	¾

*Evaluate the border fabric before purchasing it. The direction of the pattern may determine the direction in which it should be cut.

CUTTING ▶

TRADITIONAL:
Use template patterns 3a, 3b, 6h, 8m, 9a, and 9b.

QUICK:

Light-colored back-ground and navy *each*:				
2½"-wide strips	1	2	3	3
Cut strips to 2½" squares.				
2⅞"-wide strips	11	20	26	29
Cut strips to 2⅞" squares. Then cut the squares in half diagonally.				
4½"-wide strips	1	1	2	2
Cut strips to 2½" x 4½" pieces.				
8½"-wide strips	1	1	2	3
Cut strips to 4½" x 8½" pieces.				
12½"-wide strips	1	1	2	2
Cut strips to 2½" x 12½" pieces.				
8½"-wide strips	1	1	2	2
Cut strips to 2½" x 8½" pieces.				

Border fabric: If cutting the inner border lengthwise, cut those strips *before* cutting the following pieces.

12½"-wide strips	1	2	2	3
Cut strips to 2½" x 12½" pieces.				

Block One

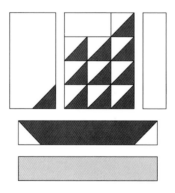

and

Step 2

Block Two

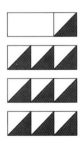

and

Step 2

Step 3

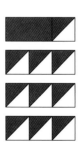

Step 3

BORDER AND BACKING:

Inner border: 6½″-wide strips:

	CRIB/WALL	TWIN	DOUBLE/QUEEN	KING
Crosswise	6	8	9	10
or Lengthwise	4	4	4	4
Backing: lengths	2	2	3	3
See piecing diagram	A	A	C	C

CONSTRUCTION

1. Make ten half-square triangle units for each block. Check for accuracy: each unit should measure 2½″.

2. If using quick-cutting and piecing methods, use the double half-square triangle technique to make the units, as shown.

3. Unit construction: see diagram.

4. Block sew order: see diagram.

5. Lay out all the blocks, alternating Block One and Block Two. Then sew the blocks together in a straight set. Refer to Chapter 5 for specific instructions.

6. Attach the inner border strips.

NOTE: The top and bottom strips were attached before the side strips on the sample quilt.

7. Make half-square triangle units for the double sawtooth border. Then sew the pieced border to the sides to complete the quilt top.

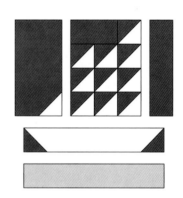

Step 4   *Step 4*

Steps 5–7

WILD GOOSE CHASE

11½" block, diagonal set with alternate blocks

Gai Perry

	CRIB/WALL	TWIN	DOUBLE/QUEEN	KING
Finished size	*49" x 49"*	*65" x 81"**	*81" x 98"**	*98" x 98"*
Blocks set	3 x 3	4 x 5	5 x 6	6 x 6
Pieced blocks	9	20	30	36
Alternate blocks	4	12	20	25
Side triangles	8	14	18	20

*Finished sizes are slightly smaller than required bed size. Borders can be added if desired. Be sure to adjust backing fabric accordingly.

YARDAGE ◀

Pieced blocks: fabrics to total	2⅛	4⅜	6¼	7½
Alternate blocks, side and corner triangles	1⅝	3	4⅜	5½
Backing	3	4	5¾	8½
Binding	⅜	½	½	⅝

CUTTING ◀

TRADITIONAL:
Use template patterns 1m, 5c, 5h, and 9d.

QUICK:
Templates are not required for quick-cutting. They are included simply to identify shapes.

Pieced blocks:				
(9d), 2⅛"-wide strips	8	17	26	31
Cut strips to 2⅛" squares.				
(9d), 2½"-wide strips	4	8	12	14
Cut strips to 2½" squares. Then cut the squares in half diagonally.				
(1m), 2¾"-wide strips*	3	7	10	12
Cut strips to 2¾" squares.*				
(5h), 3¾"-wide strips	5	10	15	18
Cut strips to 2⅛" x 3¾" pieces.				
(5c), 8⅛"-wide strips	2	4	6	8
Cut strips to 8⅛" squares. Then cut the squares into quarters diagonally.				

ALSO NEEDED:

Alternate blocks:				
12" squares	4	12	20	25
Side triangles:				
18" squares	2	4	5	5
Cut each square into quarters diagonally.				

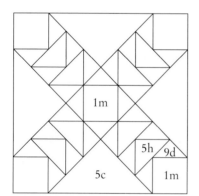

11-1/2" block

	CRIB/WALL	TWIN	DOUBLE/QUEEN	KING
Corner triangles:				
9½″ squares	2	2	2	2
Cut each square in half diagonally.				
Backing: lengths	2	2	2	3
See piecing diagram	A	B	A	C

*Cut just slightly larger than 2¾″.

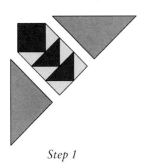

Step 1

CONSTRUCTION

1. Unit construction: see diagrams.
✂ *HELPFUL HINT*: If you are quick-piecing, use the double half-square triangle technique.

2. Block sew order: see diagram. Shapes (5c) are cut slightly too large. You may have to trim the excess fabric and straighten the edges of the blocks.

3. Lay out all the pieced blocks, alternate blocks, side and corner triangles. Then sew them together in a diagonal set. See Chapter 5 for specific instructions.

Step 2

Step 3

INTERLOCKED SQUARES

6¼" blocks

Marian Ritchie

	TWIN	QUEEN
Finished size	*68" x 94"*	*94" x 94"*
Block One	24	30
Block Two	24	36

Block One
6-1/4"

Block Two

Block Three

	TWIN	QUEEN	
Block Three	14	24	
Alternate blocks	32	49	
Pieced side triangles	10 & 10R*	12 & 12R*	*R = reverse
Solid side triangles	6	8	

YARDAGE ▶

White	5¼	6½
Navy (includes binding)	3	3¾
Backing	5½	8¼

CUTTING ▶

TRADITIONAL:
Use template patterns 6c, 6k, 11c, 11d, 11e, 11f, 11g, 11h, 11i, 11j, 11k, and 11m. There is no template pattern for the alternate block. You can make a 6¾" square from template plastic if you so desire. Templates (11i, 11j, 11k, and 11m) must be reversed for one-half of the pieced side triangles.

QUICK:
Cut border strips first. Then cut other shapes from remaining width.

White:		
6¾"-wide strips	6	9
Cut strips to 6¾" squares.		
1¾"-wide strips	30	42
Navy: 1¾"-wide strips	41	56

BORDERS AND BACKING:

White:		
Outer border: width	6½"	6½"
10⅛" squares	2	2
Cut squares into quarters diagonally.		
5¼" squares	2	2
Cut squares in half diagonally.		
Navy:		
Inner border: width	1¾"	1¾"
Backing: lengths	2	3
See piecing diagram	A	C

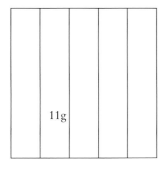

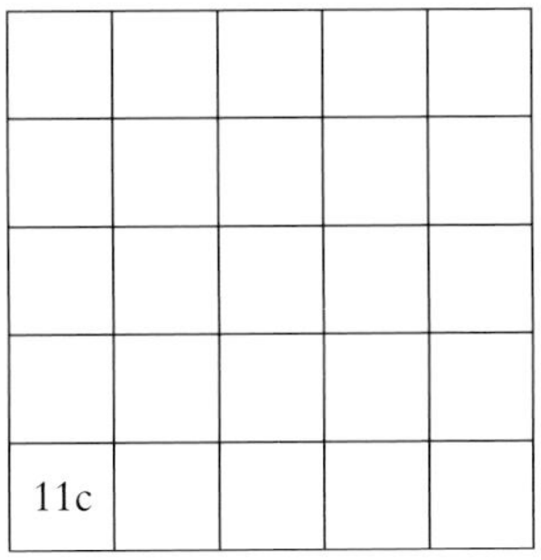

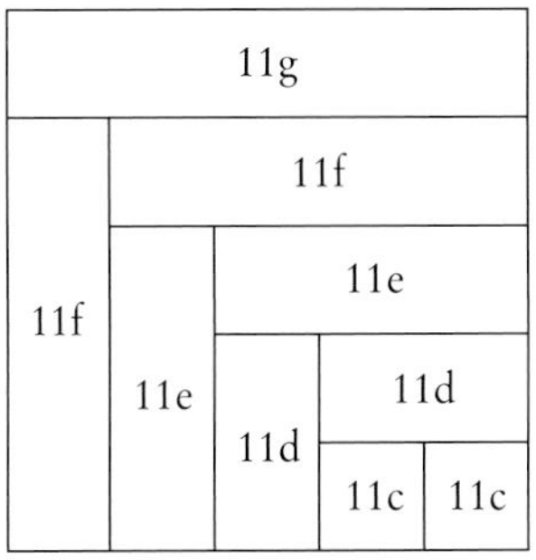

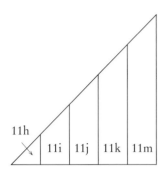

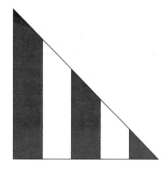

CONSTRUCTION

1. Make the required number of Block One. Sew white and navy strips together into sets. Then cut the sets apart every 6¾", as shown. Make four sets for Twin and five sets for Queen.

2. Make the required number of Block Two. Sew white and navy strips together into Set A and Set B, as shown. For Twin, make three Set A and two Set B. For Queen make Five Set A and three Set B.

3. Block sew order: see diagram.

4. Make the required number of Block Three. Sew a white and navy strip together. Then cut the set apart every 1¾", as shown. Only one set is required for each bed size.

5. Sew the units cut in Step 4 to strips of white fabric, as shown.

6. Press the seam in the direction of the white strip. Then cut the new units apart, as shown. Trim the excess fabric and straighten the edges.

7. Sew the new units to strips of navy fabric. Press and then cut the new units apart, as shown.

8. Continue adding strips in the same manner, referring to the diagrams for help.

9. Make the pieced side triangles: sew white and navy strips together into sets, exactly as done in Step 1. Use template (6k) to mark the angles. Then cut as shown.

10. Lay out all the blocks and side triangles. Then sew them together in a diagonal set. Refer to the diagram for help.

11. Attach the inner navy and then outer white border to complete the quilt top.

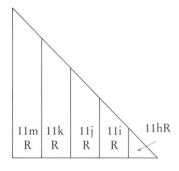

Interlocked Squares Layout

66
▼

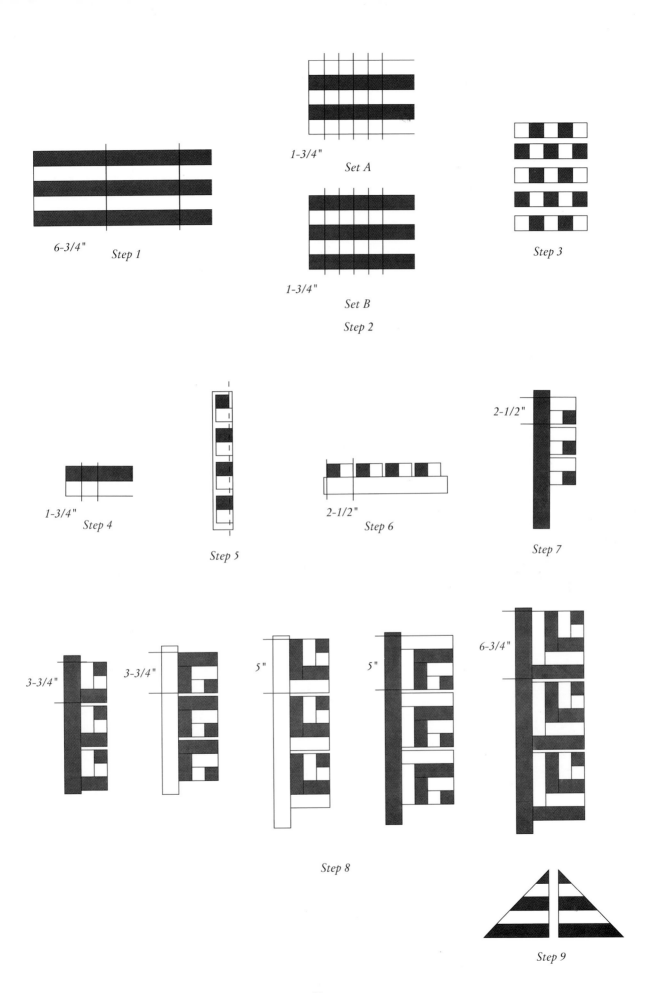

1-3/4"

Set A

6-3/4"   Step 1

Step 3

1-3/4"

Set B

Step 2

1-3/4"   Step 4

Step 5

2-1/2"

Step 6

2-1/2"

Step 7

3-3/4"   3-3/4"   5"   5"   6-3/4"

Step 8

Step 9

LADY OF THE LAKE

10″ block, straight set

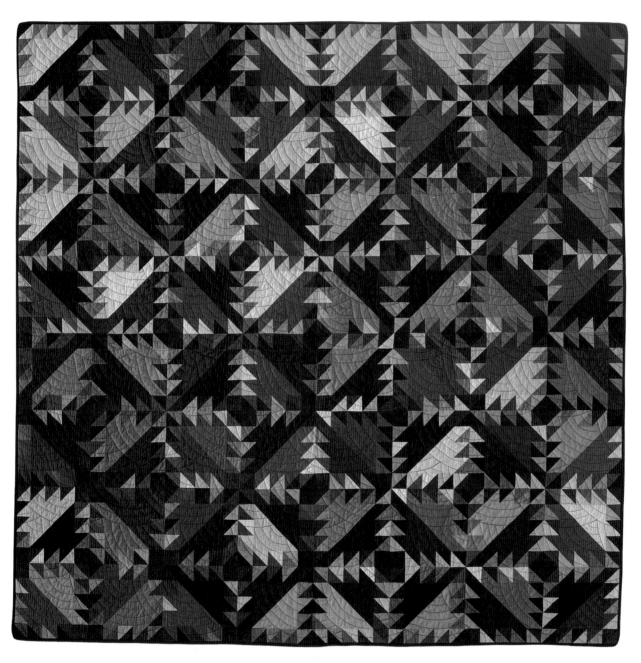

Mabry Benson

	CRIB/WALL	TWIN	DOUBLE/QUEEN	KING
Finished size	*50″ x 60″*	*70″ x 90″*	*90″ x 90″*	*100″ x 100″*
Blocks set	5 x 6	7 x 9	9 x 9	10 x 10
Total blocks	30	63	81	100

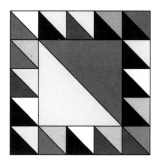

YARDAGE

Pieced blocks: light, medium, and dark				
fabrics to total	4	8¼	10¼	13
Backing	3	5½	8	8¾
Binding	⅜	½	⅝	⅝

CUTTING

TRADITIONAL:

Use template patterns 6e and 6h.

QUICK:

2⅞"-wide strips	35	72	93	115
Cut strips to 2⅞" squares. Then cut the squares in half diagonally.				
6⅞"-wide strips	5	11	14	17
Cut strips to 6⅞" squares. Then cut the squares in half diagonally.				
Backing: lengths	1	2	3	3
See piecing diagram	B	A	C	C

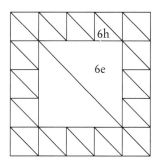

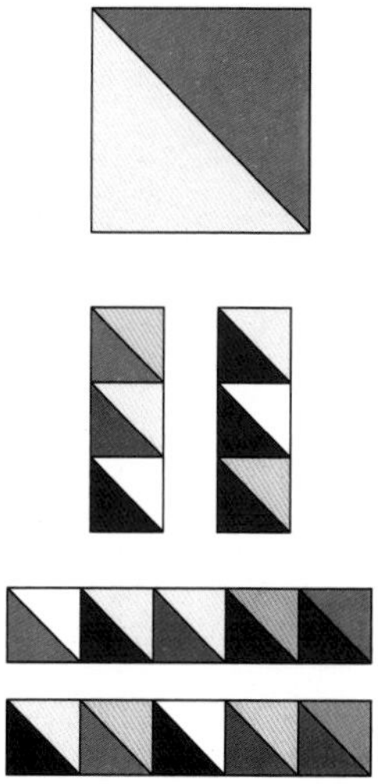

10" block

CONSTRUCTION

1. Make half-square triangle units. Make combinations of light/medium, light/dark, and medium/dark units. Check for accuracy: each unit should measure 2½".

2. Unit construction: see diagrams. Make combinations of light/medium, light/dark, and medium/dark fabrics.

3. Block sew order: see diagrams.

Position the light, medium, and dark sides of the half-square triangle units to correspond with the larger triangles. Refer to the photo for help.

4. Lay out all the blocks, alternating the direction, as shown. Then sew them together in a straight set. Refer to Chapter 5 for specific instructions.

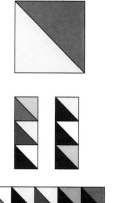

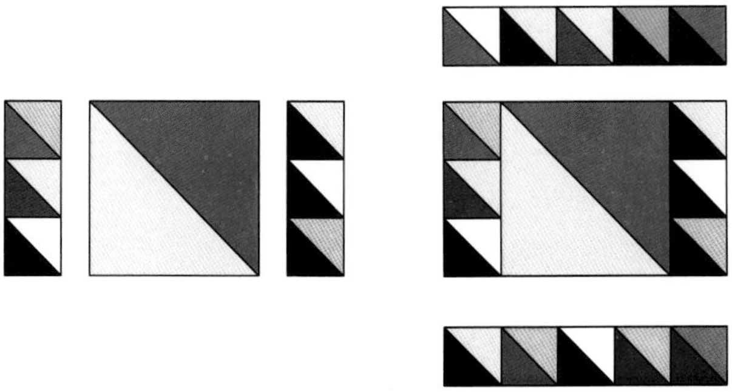

Step 2

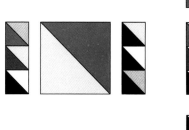

Step 3

Step 4

ROW HOUSE

12" block, straight set

Diana McClun and Laura Nownes; quilted by Anna Venti

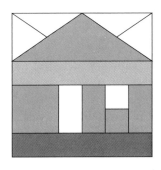

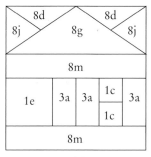

12" block

	CRIB/WALL	TWIN	DOUBLE/QUEEN	KING
Finished size	*76" x 38"*	*76" x 86"*	*88" x 98"*	*112" x 110"*
Blocks set	6 x 3	6 x 7	7 x 8	9 x 9
Total blocks	18	42	56	81

YARDAGE ◄

Sky	⅜	¾	1⅛	1⅜
Mountains	⅜	¾	1	1¼
Roofs: fabrics to total	½	1¼	1½	2⅛
Eaves: fabrics to total	¾	1⅛	1½	2¼
House fronts: fabrics to total	1	1¾	2⅜	3⅛
Doors: fabrics to total	⅜	½	⅝	⅞
Windows: fabrics to total	¼	¼	⅜	½
Ground: fabrics to total	⅞	1⅛	1⅝	2⅛
Backing	2¼	5	8	9½
Binding	⅜	⅝	¾	¾

CUTTING ►

TRADITIONAL:

Use template patterns 1c, 1e, 3a, 8d, 8g, 8j, 8m, and 8n. ✄ *HELPFUL HINT*: Remember to transfer the dots from (8d, 8g, and 8j) onto the fabric shapes.

QUICK:

To achieve a scrap look similar to the sample quilt, make each block different. Strip cutting is given for only those fabrics which are consistent throughout the blocks (sky and mountain). Otherwise individual shapes, sizes, and amounts are given.

Sky: 2⅝"-wide strips	4	10	13	18
Use with (8d) to mark angles for cutting.				
Mountains: 3¾"-wide strips	3	6	8	11
Use with (8j) to mark angles for cutting.				
Roofs: use (8g)	18	42	56	81
Eaves: 2½" x 12½" pieces	18	42	56	81
House fronts: 2½" squares	18	42	56	81
2½" x 4½" pieces	36	84	112	162
4½" squares	18	42	56	81
Doors: 2½" x 4½" pieces	18	42	56	81
Windows: 2½" squares	18	42	56	81
Ground: 2½" x 12½" pieces	18	42	56	81

BORDER AND BACKING:

Border (top and sides):				
2½" x 12½" pieces	8	16	19	23
2½" x 14½" pieces	2	2	2	2
Backing: lengths	1	2	3	3
See piecing diagram	—	A	D	C

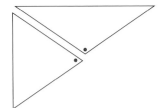

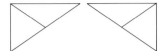

Step 1

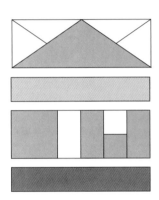

Step 2

Step 3

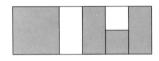

Step 4

CONSTRUCTION

1. Transfer the dots from the template pattern onto the plastic and then to the fabric shape. Sew the sky shapes to the mountain shapes, matching the dots, as shown. Press the seams in the direction of the mountain shape.

2. Sew the sky/mountain units to the roof, matching the seamlines with the dots on the roof, as shown.

3. Sew the house front pieces, door and window shapes, as shown.

4. Block sew order: see diagram.

5. Lay out all the blocks. Then sew them together in a straight set. Refer to Chapter 5 for specific instructions.

6. Sew enough 2½" x 12½" pieces together for the top edge of the quilt. Then sew them to the quilt.

7. Sew enough border pieces together for the sides of the quilt. NOTE: The top border piece on each side is 2½" x 14½". All other border pieces are 2½" x 12½". Sew these pieces to the sides to complete the quilt top.

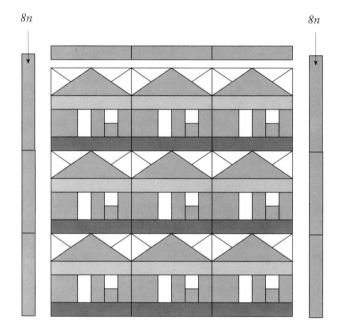

Steps 6–7

PINE TREES

12″ block, streak of lightning set

Diana McClun and Laura Nownes; quilted by JoAnn Manning

	TWIN	DOUBLE/QUEEN
Finished size★	*60″ x 60″*	*94″ x 94″*
Vertical rows	3	5
Whole blocks	8	23
Half blocks	2	4
Large triangles	14	44
Small triangles	8	12

★This set with a 12″ block does not lend itself to all bed sizes.

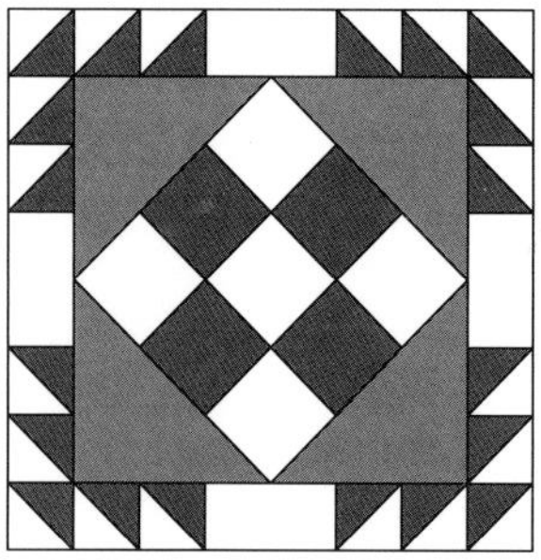

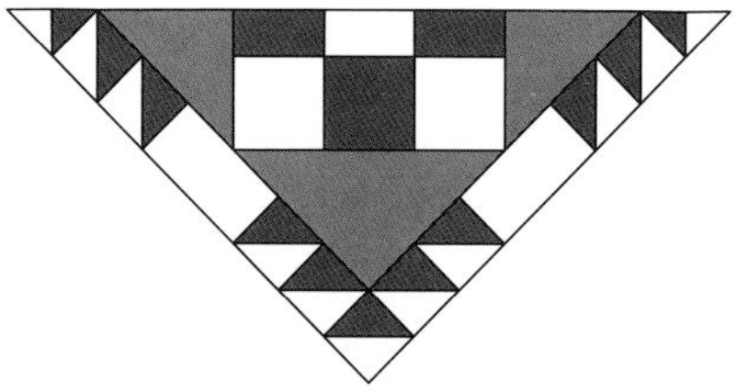

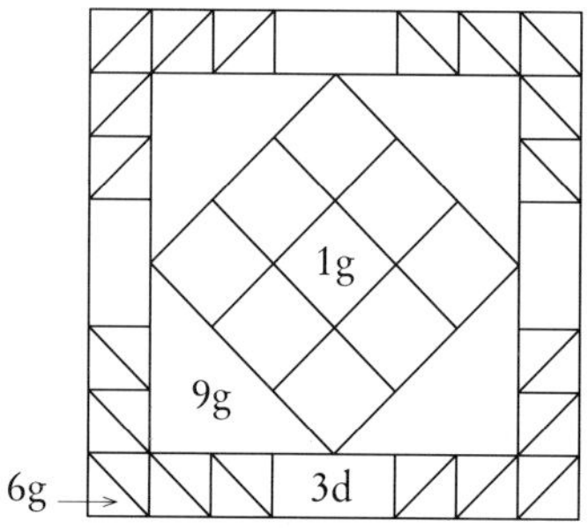

12" block

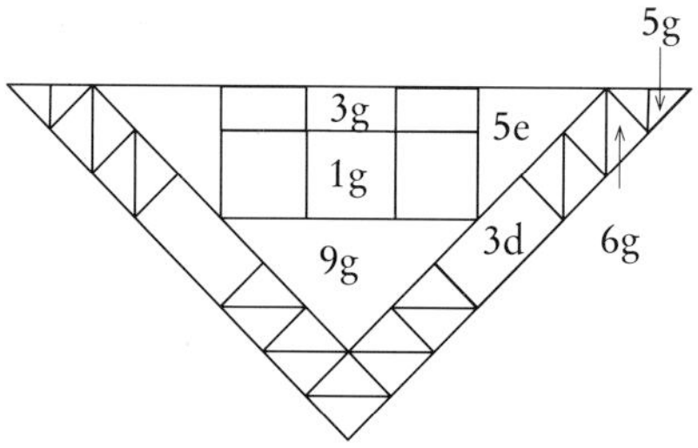

Pine Trees half-block
12" block

YARDAGE

	TWIN	DOUBLE/QUEEN
Light-colored background	1½	3½
Greens (pieced blocks): fabrics to total	1½	2¾
Green (setting triangles, border and binding)	3	5¾
Backing	3⅝	8½

CUTTING

TRADITIONAL:

Use template patterns 1g, 3d, 3g, 5e, 5g, 6g, and 9g. There are no template patterns for the large and small green setting triangles. Refer to quick-cutting instructions for sizes.

QUICK:

NOTE: Templates are not required for quick-cutting. They are included simply to identify shapes.

Light-colored background: Cut border strips first (see below). Then use remaining width to cut other shapes.

	TWIN	DOUBLE/QUEEN
(6g), 2⅜″-wide strips	10	26
Cut strips to 2⅜″ squares. Then cut the squares in half diagonally.		
(1g), 2⅝″-wide strips	3	8
(3d), 3½″-wide strips	3	8
Cut strips to 2″ x 3½″ pieces.		
(5g), 2¾″ squares	1	2
Cut the squares into quarters diagonally.		
(3g), 1⅝″ x 2⅝″ pieces	2	4
Greens (pieced blocks):		
(6g), 2⅜″-wide strips	6	16
Cut strips to 2⅜″ squares. Then cut the squares in half diagonally.		
(1g), 2⅝″-wide strips	3	8
(9g), 5⅜″-wide strips	3	7
Cut strips to 5⅜″ squares. Then cut the squares in half diagonally.		
(5g), 2¾″ squares	1	2
Cut the squares into quarters diagonally.		
(3g), 1⅝″ x 2⅝″ pieces	4	8
(5e), 5¾″ squares	1	2
Cut the squares into quarters diagonally.		
Green (setting triangles):		
Cut border strips first (see below). Then use the remaining width to cut the setting triangles.		
18½″ squares	4	11
Cut squares into quarters diagonally (large triangles).		

Set A

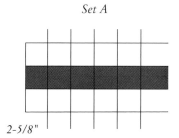

2-5/8"

Set B

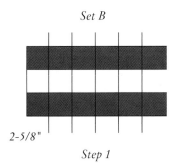

2-5/8"

Step 1

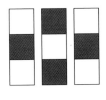

Step 2

Make two for each block:

and

Then, make two for each block:

and two for each block:

Step 4

	TWIN	DOUBLE/QUEEN
10" squares	4	6
Cut squares in half diagonally (small triangles).		
BORDERS AND BACKING:		
Light-colored background:		
2"-wide strips	9	9
(Use one strip for pieced corner blocks.)		
Green:		
2"-wide strips	5	5
(Use one strip for pieced corner blocks.)		
Backing: lengths	2	3
See piecing diagram	A	C

CONSTRUCTION

1. Sew light-colored and green 2⅝"-wide strips together in sets. Then cut the sets apart every 2⅝", as shown.

The following chart is based on 24" lengths of light-colored fabric (width of fabric remaining after cutting border strips).

	TWIN	DOUBLE/QUEEN
Set A	3	6
Set B	2	3

2. Unit construction: see diagram.
3. Make half-square triangle units. You will need twenty for each block.

Check for accuracy: each unit should measure 2".

4. Unit construction: see diagrams.
5. Block sew order: see diagrams.

✄ *HELPFUL HINT*: It is easier to use full-size shapes for the half-blocks, then trim the excess. Remember to allow the ¼" seam allowance along the diagonal edge.

6. Lay out all the pieced blocks and setting triangles. Then sew them together in a streak of lightning set. Refer to Chapter 5 for specific instructions.

Step 5

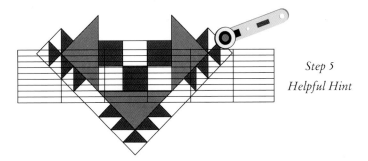

Step 5
Helpful Hint

75

APPLE BASKET

12" block, straight set with horizontal sashing

Diana McClun and Laura Nownes; quilted by Anna Venti

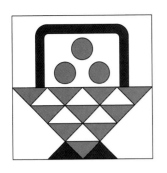

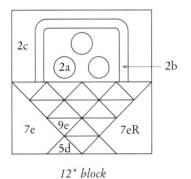

12" block

	CRIB/WALL	TWIN	DOUBLE/QUEEN	KING
Finished size	*47″ x 55″*	*71″ x 87″*	*95″ x 103″*	*107″ x 103″*
Blocks set	3 x 9	5 x 5	7 x 6	8 x 6
Total blocks	9	25	42	48
Border units	50	76	96	100

YARDAGE ◄

Light-colored background	2	4¼	5¾	6½
Greens (basket): fabrics to total	1⅛	1⅞	2⅝	2⅞
Red	⅛	¼	⅜	⅜
Dark green (handles, borders and binding)	1½	2¾	3½	3½
Apples	⅛	⅜	½	⅝
Floral sashing: Crosswise	⅜	¾	1½	1¾
or Lengthwise	1⅛	1¾	2½	2¾
Backing	2⅞	5	8	8¾

CUTTING ◄

TRADITIONAL:

Use template patterns 2a, 2b, 2c, 5d, 7e, and 9e. ☞ *WARNING*: Remember to reverse the direction for one-half of the (7e) shapes.

QUICK:

Light-colored background: 3″-wide strips	10	17	23	25

Cut strips to 3″ squares. Then cut the squares in half diagonally.

6⅞″-wide strips	2	5	7	8

Cut strips to 6⅞″ squares. Then cut the squares in half diagonally. Use (7e) to mark the angle for cutting. ☞ *WARNING*: One-half of the shapes must be reversed.

12½″-wide strips	2	5	7	8

Cut strips to 6½″ x 12½″ pieces.

Greens: 3″-wide strips	11	19	28	30

Cut strips to 3″ squares. Then cut the squares in half diagonally.

Red: 4¼″-wide strips	1	2	3	3

Cut strips to 4¼″ squares. Then cut the squares into quarters diagonally.

ALSO NEEDED:				
Apples: use (2a)	27	75	126	144
Handles: use (2b)	9	25	42	48
SASHING, BORDERS, AND BACKING:				
Dark green:				
Inner and outer border:				
width	2"	2"	2"	2"
Floral sashing: width	4½"	4½"	4½"	4½"
Backing: lengths	2	2	3	3
See piecing diagram	B	A	D	C

Step 3

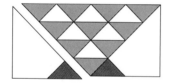

Step 4

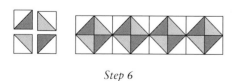

Step 6

CONSTRUCTION

1. Use one of the appliqué techniques in Chapter 4 to appliqué a handle and three apples in each large light-colored background piece.

2. Make half-square triangle units. You will need six for each block. Check for accuracy: each unit should measure 2⅛".

3. Unit construction: see diagrams.

4. Block sew order: see diagrams.

5. Lay out all the blocks. Then sew them together in a straight set, separating each horizontal row with a sashing strip.

6. Make half-square triangles for pieced border. Sew four together for each unit. Then join the units together, as shown.

7. Attach an inner border strip to two opposite sides of the quilt top. Then attach two pieced border strips to the same two sides, as shown.

8. Attach an inner border strip to the top and bottom edges of the quilt top. Then attach pieced border strips, joining a short strip of inner border fabric at each corner unit, as shown. NOTE: You may need to adjust the width of the inner border strips to make the pieced borders fit perfectly.

9. Attach the outer border strips to complete the quilt top.

Steps 7–8

COURTHOUSE SQUARE

12" block, straight set

Diana McClun and Laura Nownes; quilted by Kathy Sandbach

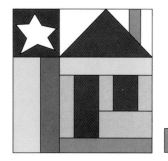

	CRIB/WALL	TWIN	DOUBLE/QUEEN	KING
Finished size	45" x 57"	69" x 93"	93" x 93"	105" x93"
Blocks set	3 x 4	5 x 7	7 x 7	8 x 7
Total blocks	12	35	49	56

YARDAGE ▶

	CRIB/WALL	TWIN	DOUBLE/QUEEN	KING
Stars	¼	½	⅝	¾
Black (star background)	¼	½	¾	⅞
Flags (stripe)	¼	¾	1	1
Flags (red)	¼	½	¾	¾
Sky	¼	½	¾	¾
Chimneys: fabrics to total	⅛	¼	¼	¼
Roofs: fabrics to total	⅜	1	1⅛	1⅛
Eaves: fabrics to total	¼	½	¾	¾
House fronts and pieced border: fabrics to total	½	1	1¾	1¾
Doors: fabrics to total	¼	⅝	¾	¾
Windows: fabrics to total	⅛	⅜	⅝	⅝
Ground: fabrics to total	⅜	⅝	⅞	⅞
Gold (inner and pieced borders):				
Crosswise	⅞	1⅛	1⅜	1⅜
or Lengthwise	1½	2½	2½	2⅞
Black print (pieced border)	½	⅝	¾	¾
Black (outer border):				
Crosswise	⅜	½	⅝	⅝
or Lengthwise	1¾	2¾	2¾	3
Backing	2⅞	5½	8¼	8¼
Binding	⅜	½	⅝	⅝

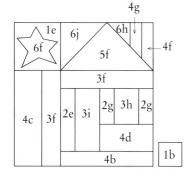

12" block

CUTTING ▶

TRADITIONAL:
Use template patterns 1b, 1e, 2e, 2g, 3f, 3h, 3i, 4b, 4c, 4d, 4f, 4g, 5f, 6f, 6h, and 6j.

QUICK:
You will probably want a scrap look similar to our sample quilt. Strip cutting is given only for those fabrics which are consistent throughout the blocks. Otherwise, individual shape sizes and amounts are given. With the exception of the star and the roof, templates are not required for quick-cutting; they are included only to identify shapes.

	CRIB/WALL	TWIN	DOUBLE/QUEEN	KING
Stars: use (6f)	12	35	49	56
Star background (1e): 4½"-wide strips	2	4	6	7
Cut strips to 4½" squares.				
Flags (stripe) (4c): 3"-wide strips	3	9	13	14

Flags (red) (3f):				
2″-wide strips	3	9	13	14
Sky (6j):				
4⅞″-wide strips	2	5	7	7
Cut strips to 4⅞″ squares. Then cut the squares in half diagonally.				
Chimneys (4g):				
1½″-wide strips	1	2	2	2
Cut strips to 1½″ x 3⅞″ pieces.				
Roofs: use (5f)	12	35	49	56
Eaves (3f):				
2″ x 8½″ pieces	12	35	49	56
House front:				
(2g), 1¾″ x 3½″ pieces	24	70	98	112
(4d), 2¾″ x 5⅛″ pieces	12	35	49	56
(2e), 1¾″ x 5¾″ pieces	12	35	49	56
Doors (3i):				
2⅝″ x 5¾″ pieces	12	35	49	56
Windows (3h):				
2⅝″ x 3½″ pieces	12	35	49	56
Ground (4b):				
1¾″ x 8½″ pieces	12	35	49	56
BORDERS AND BACKING:				
Gold (inner and pieced borders): 2″-wide strips				
Crosswise	12	18	20	21
or Lengthwise	10	10	11	12
Black (pieced border):				
2″-wide strips	7	10	11	12
Red (pieced border):				
2″-wide strips	1	2	3	3
Black (outer border):				
2″-wide strips				
Crosswise	6	8	10	11
or Lengthwise	4	4	4	4
Backing: lengths	2	2	3	3
See piecing diagram	B	A	C	C

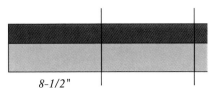

8-1/2"

Step 2

Step 3

CONSTRUCTION

1. Appliqué a star to each star background square. See Chapter 4 for specific appliqué instructions.

2. Join the flag stripe and red fabric strips in pairs. Then cut the sets apart every 8½", as shown.

3. Sky/chimney unit: If you are quick-piecing, you can simply fold the sides of the chimney shape ¼" to the wrong side and press. Then position the chimney onto the sky triangle and either hand applique or machine stitch along the edges, as shown. Then trim the excess length of chimney fabric.

4. Unit construction: see diagrams.

5. Block sew order: see diagrams.

6. Lay out all the blocks. Then sew them together in a straight set. Refer to Chapter 5 for specific instructions.

7. Attach the inner gold border.

8. Use 2"-wide strips of black, gold, and red fabrics to make four-patch blocks, as shown.

9. Join blocks to make pieced border strips. Then attach the strips to the sides to complete the quilt top, as shown.

Step 4

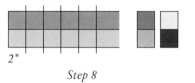

2"

Step 8

Step 5

Step 9

MARTHA WASHINGTON STAR

12" block, straight set with sashing

Diana McClun and Laura Nownes; quilted by Kathy Sandbach

	CRIB/WALL	TWIN	DOUBLE/QUEEN	KING
Finished size	*47" x 60"*	*73" x 85"*	*85" x 98"*	*98" x 98"*
Blocks set	3 x 4	5 x 6	6 x 7	8 x 8
Total blocks	12	30	42	64

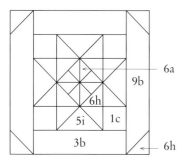

12" block

YARDAGE

	CRIB/WALL	TWIN	DOUBLE/QUEEN	KING
Black	2	4¼	5⅞	8¼
Pieced blocks and pieced borders: fabrics to total	2½	4½	5¼	7¼
Sashing and inner border:				
Crosswise	½	1	1¼	1½
or Lengthwise	1¾	2½	3	3
Corners: two fabrics *each*	¼	⅜	½	⅝
Backing	3	5	7½	8½
Binding	⅜	½	½	⅝

CUTTING

TRADITIONAL:
Use template patterns 1c, 3b, 5i, 6a, 6h, and 9b.

QUICK:
NOTE: Templates are not required for quick-cutting. They are included simply to identify shapes.

	CRIB/WALL	TWIN	DOUBLE/QUEEN	KING
Black: (1c), 2½″-wide strips	3	8	11	16
Cut to 2½″ squares.				
(5i), 4½″-wide strips	3	8	11	16
Cut strips to 2½″x 4½″ pieces.				
(3b), 8½″-wide strips	2	4	6	8
Cut strips to 2½″ x 8½″ pieces.				
(9b), 12½″-wide strips	2	4	6	8
Cut strips to 2½″ x 12½″ pieces.				
Pieced blocks and pieced border:				
(6h), 2½″-wide strips	6	15	21	32
Cut strips to 2½″ squares.				
(6h), 2⅞″-wide strips	9	16	18	24
Cut strips to 2⅞″ squares. Then cut the squares in half diagonally.				
(6a), 2¼″-wide strips	11	19	21	28
Cut strips to 2¼″ squares. Then cut the squares in half diagonally.				
Corners, two fabrics *each*:				
(6h), 2½″-wide strips	2	4	6	8
Cut strips to 2½″ squares.				

SASHING, BORDER, AND BACKING:

	CRIB/WALL	TWIN	DOUBLE/QUEEN	KING
Sashing and inner border: width	1¼″*	1¼″*	1¼″*	1¼″*
Backing: lengths	2	2	3	3
See piecing diagram	B	A	D	C

*Cut the border strips *after* constructing the pieced border. You may need to adjust the width of the strips to attach the pieced border successfully.

Step 1

CONSTRUCTION

1. Make the required number of pieced blocks. If you are quick-piecing, use the double half-square triangle technique, as shown. Unit construction: see diagrams.

2. If you are quick-piecing, use the double half-square triangle technique to attach the corners to the black 2½″ x 12½″ pieces. Position color one and color two as shown.

3. Block sew order: see diagrams.

4. Lay out all the blocks. Sew them together in a straight set with sashing strips. See Chapter 5 for specific instructions.

5. Make the pieced border units. Refer to the first two diagrams in Step 1 for help.

6. Join border units to make the length of the sides of the quilt.

7. Cut the inner border strips, adjusting the width as necessary to make the pieced border fit. Refer to Chapter 5 for help.

8. Attach the inner border and then pieced border to complete the quilt top.

Color one   *Color two*

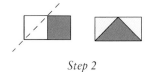

Step 2

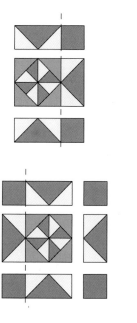

Steps 4–8

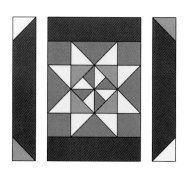

Step 3

STAR OF BETHLEHEM

Diana McClun and Laura Nownes; quilted by JoAnn Manning

	CRIB/WALL	TWIN	DOUBLE/QUEEN	KING
Finished size	63″ x 63″	81″ x 81″	85″ x 85″	100″ x 100″
Star size	51″	69″	69″	84″

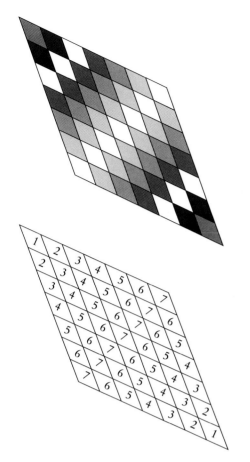

YARDAGE

Star and pieced border:

Fabric 1	⅜	½	⅝	¾
Fabric 2	⅜	⅝	⅝	⅞
Fabric 3	½	¾	¾	1
Fabric 4	⅝	⅞	1	1¼
Fabric 5	¾	1	1	1½
Fabric 6	⅞	1	1⅛	1½
Fabric 7	⅝	¾	⅞	1⅛
Background	3½	4½	5½	6½
Backing	4	4¾	7½	8¾
Binding	⅜	½	½	⅝

CUTTING

☞ *WARNING*: These charts differ from all the others in the book. Please read through them carefully *before* cutting to avoid errors. Cut the corner squares and side triangles from the background fabric *before* cutting shapes for the pieced border. Accuracy in cutting and sewing is important for a neat, flat quilt.

TRADITIONAL:

Use template patterns:
• For Crib/Wall: 5j, 5d, and 6g
• For Twin: 5k, 5d, and 6g
• For Double/Queen: 5k, 5i, and 6h
• For King: 5m, 5i, and 6h

QUICK:

The following chart indicates the number of strips to cut from *each* star fabric. Strip widths are as follows:
• For Crib/Wall: 2″-wide
• For Twin, Double, and Queen: 2½″-wide
• For King: 3″-wide

Fabric 1	2	2	2	2
Fabric 2	3	3	3	4
Fabric 3	5	5	5	6
Fabric 4	7	7	7	8
Fabric 5	8	8	8	10
Fabric 6	10	10	10	12
Fabric 7	6	6	6	7

Pieced border: Strip widths are as follows:
• For Crib/ Wall and Twin: 3½″-wide strips. Cut strips to 2″ x 3½″ pieces.
• For Double/Queen and King: 4½″-wide strips. Cut strips to 2½″ x 4½″ pieces.

Cut the following number of strips from *each* fabric for the pieced border.

Fabrics 1-7 *each*	2	3	3	4
Background:				
Corner squares, four	18″	23″	24″	28″
Side triangles, one square	25″	33″	34″	39″

Cut the square into quarters diagonally.

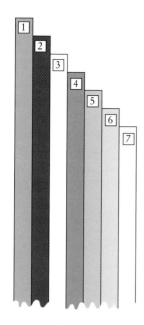

Step 1
Strip sequence for Set One

	CRIB/WALL	TWIN	DOUBLE/QUEEN	KING
Pieced border:				
2″-wide strips	29	38	—	—
Cut strips to 2″ squares.				
2½″-wide strips	—	—	37	45
Cut strips to 2½″ squares.				
Backing: lengths	2	2	3	3
See piecing diagram	A	A	C	C

CONSTRUCTION

Strip sequence for sets:
Set One: 1-2-3-4-5-6-7
Set Two: 2-3-4-5-6-7-6
Set Three: 3-4-5-6-7-6-5
Set Four: 4-5-6-7-6-5-4

Number of sets:				
Set One	1½	1½	1½	2
Set Two	1½	1½	1½	2
Set Three	1½	1½	1½	2
Set Four	1	1	1	1

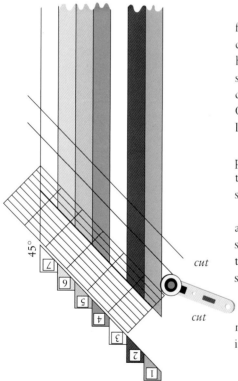

Steps 2–3

1. Make the required number of sets for the size quilt you are making: see diagram. ✄ *HELPFUL HINT*:To make half-sets, cut the strips in half before sewing into sets. Note the drop in successive strips. Make a 1½″ drop for Crib/Wall, a 2″ drop for Twin and Double/Queen, and a 2½″ drop for King.

2. Line the 45° angle on your wide plastic ruler with the left-hand edge of the set of strips. Then trim the edges, as shown.

3. Continue cutting units of strips along the full length of the set, as shown. The distance between cuts is the same measurement used to cut the strips (2″, 2½″, or 3″).

4. Unit construction: see diagrams.

5. Star sew order: see diagrams. Do not stitch into the seam allowances, as indicated by dots in the diagram. The large background pieces of the center star are cut slightly too big, to allow for straightening the edges and making any necessary adjustment when you attach the pieced border.

6. Make border units: if you are quick piecing, use the double half-square triangle technique, using the 2½″ squares of background and 2½″ x 4½″ pieces of other fabrics. Join the units together, as shown.

7. Lay the pieced border strips along the edges of the quilt top to determine how much excess background must be removed in order to allow the borders to fit properly. Then trim the excess, making certain that corners are accurate 90° angles.

8. Attach the pieced borders to complete the quilt top.

Set One   1 2 3 4 5 6 7

Set Two   2 3 4 5 6 7 6

Set Three   3 4 5 6 7 6 5

Set Four   4 5 6 7 6 5 4

Set Three R   5 6 7 6 5 4 3

Set Two R   6 7 6 5 4 3 2

Set One R   7 6 5 4 3 2 1

Make eight.
Step 4

Make four.
Step 5

Step 6

Sides

Corners: make four.

Step 5

SIX-POINTED STAR VARIATION

14" x 12" units

Diana McClun and Laura Nownes; quilted by JoAnn Manning

Unit One

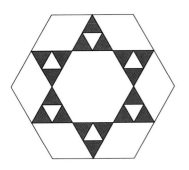

Unit Two

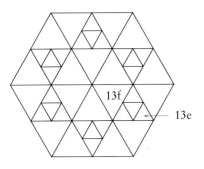

Unit One

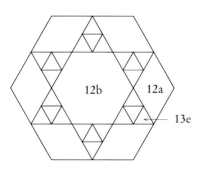

Unit Two

	CRIB/WALL	TWIN	DOUBLE/QUEEN	KING
Finished size	46" x 66"	74" x 90"	87" x 90"	101" x 102"
Units set	3 x 5	5 x 7	6 x 7	7 x 8
Unit One	10	23	28	37
Unit Two	3	9	11	15
Side units	4	6	6	8

YARDAGE ◀

Light-colored back- ground	2⅛	3¾	4¼	5¼
Blues: fabrics to total	2⅛	4¼	4¾	6
Pink	1¾	3	3⅜	4½
Backing	3	5½	8	9
Binding	⅜	½	½	⅝

CUTTING ◀

TRADITIONAL:
Use template patterns 13a, 13e, 13f, 14a, 14b, and 14c. ☞ *WARNING*: Remember to reverse the cutting direction for one-half of the (13a) shapes.

QUICK:
With template patterns 13a, 13e, 13f, 14b, and 14c.

Light-colored background:				
2¼"-wide strips	3	8	9	12
Use (13e) to mark angles for cutting.				
3¾"-wide strips	6	14	16	21
Use (13f) to mark angles for cutting.				
3½"-wide strips	2	6	8	10
Use (14c) to mark angles for cutting.				
3½"-wide strips	4	6	6	7
Cut strips to 2" x 3½" pieces.				
2" squares	4	4	4	4
Blues:				
2¼"-wide strips	9	22	26	34
Use (13e) to mark angles for cutting.				
3¾"-wide strips	6	14	16	21
Use (13f) to mark angles for cutting.				
2"-wide strips	15	21	23	26
Cut strips to 2" squares.				

Pink:
Cut inner border (adjustment strip) before cutting other shapes. Number of strips for other shapes are based on 30" remaining width of fabric.

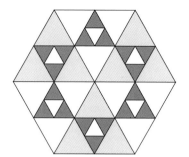

Unit One

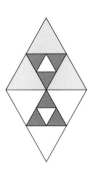

Unit Two

Side Unit

	CRIB/WALL	TWIN	DOUBLE/QUEEN	KING
3½″-wide strips	4	6	6	7
Cut strips to 2″ x 3½″ pieces.				
4¼″-wide strip	1	1	1	1
Use (13a) to mark angles for cutting. Reverse the direction on one-half of the shapes.				
6¾″-wide strips	4	11	13	18
Use (14b) to mark angles for cutting.				

✂ *HELPFUL HINT*: Indicate the side with straight grain on a piece of paper pinned to the triangles, as it will be important during construction.

ALSO NEEDED:

	CRIB/WALL	TWIN	DOUBLE/QUEEN	KING
Light-colored background: use (14a)	3	9	11	15
Pink:				
Inner border: width	3″	3″	3″	3″
Backing: lengths	2	2	3	3
See piecing diagram	B	A	C	C

CONSTRUCTION

1. For all units: make six for each of Units One and Two and two for each Side Unit. ✂ *HELPFUL HINT*: Do not cut the extensions from the triangles until the entire unit is constructed, as they help in lining up the triangles for sewing.

2. Unit construction: see diagrams. Make three each for Unit Ones and one each for Side Units.

3. Unit One: see sew order diagram.

4. Side unit: see sew order diagram.

5. Unit Two: sew the remaining shapes made in Step 1 to (14a) and (14c), as shown.

6. Join all units together in rows, referring to the diagram for help. Place the straight grain on the large pink setting triangles, as indicated by the arrows, to keep the rows from stretching.

7. Join the horizontal rows.

8. Make units for the pieced border, as shown. If you are quick-piecing, use the double half-square triangle technique.

9. Join units together and lay them out along the edges of the quilt top. Then attach the pink inner border strips, adjusting the width as necessary, to make the pieced border fit.

Step 1

Step 2

Step 3

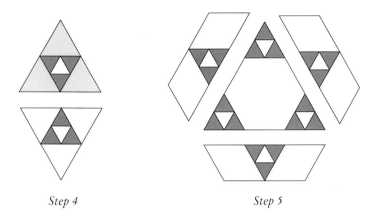

Step 4   *Step 5*

Step 6

and

Step 8

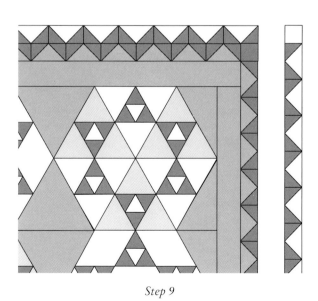

Step 9

▼

FOLKART MEDALLION

16" center appliqué medallion

An original design by Claire Jarratt adapted from an antique Baltimore Album block

Claire Jarratt and friends; quilted by Claire Jarratt

16" block

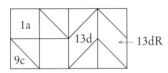

Zigzag border

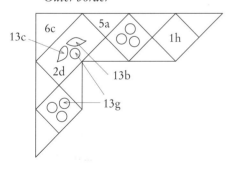

Outer border

Finished size | 38" x 38"

YARDAGE

Light-colored background	1¾
Red (includes binding)	2
Light green (vine and leaves)	⅝
Dark green (leaves)	⅛
Blue print	½

Also: variety of green, brown, blue, red, and yellow scraps for center appliqué medallion.

CUTTING

TRADITIONAL:
Use appliqué medallion pattern (end of book) and template patterns 1a, 1h, 2d, 5a, 6c, 9c, 13b, 13c, 13d, and 13g. ☞ *WARNING*: Remember to reverse the direction for one-half the (13d) shapes.

QUICK:
Center Medallion:
Light-colored background: One 17½" square
Use a variety of scraps for the shapes in the center appliqué medallion.
Zigzag border:

Light-colored background: 1½"-wide strips	5
Cut strips to 1½" squares.	
Red: 2½"-wide strips	3
Cut strips to 1½" x 2½" pieces.	
Background and red, layered: 1⅞"-wide strips, *each*	4
Cut strips to 1⅞" squares. Then cut each square in half diagonally.	
Vine border:	
Light-colored background: 3½" x 21½" pieces	2
3½" x 26" pieces	2
Light green:	
Cut ¾" bias strips, pieced to approximately 112". Fold under to finish ¼" wide.	
Light, medium, and dark green: use (13b and 13c)	25
Cherries: use (13g)	3
Red border:	
1½" x 26½" pieces	2
1½" x 28½" pieces	2
Cherry appliqué border:	
Light-colored background:	
3¼" squares	24
Red: use (13g)	76
Dark green: (13b and 13c), *each*	4

Blue print: 5½″ squares   16

Cut two squares in half diagonally (for corners).
   Then cut the remaining squares into quarters
   diagonally (for sides).

Sawtooth border:

Light-colored background and red, layered:

1⅞″-wide strips, *each*   4

Cut strips to 1⅞″ squares. Then cut the squares
   in half diagonally.

1½″ squares, *each*   2

Zigzag border

                Make four corner units.

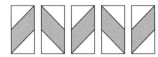

Make four sets of sixteen each.

Step 2

CONSTRUCTION

1. Use one of the appliqué techniques described in Chapter 4 for the center medallion. Then trim the completed block to 16½″.

2. Zigzag border: unit construction, see diagrams. If quick-piecing, use double half-square triangle technique with the 1½″ light background squares and 1½″ x 2½″ red pieces.

3. Attach the zigzag border to the center appliqué block.

4. Attach the 3½″-wide strips of light-colored background fabric. Then appliqué the vine and leaves. Three red cherries have also been included in this border.

5. Attach the red 1½″-wide border strips.

6. Outer pieced border: unit construction, see diagrams. Side and corner triangles are cut slightly too big. Straighten the edges and remove the excess to within ⅜″ of the corners of the squares and rectangles.

7. Attach the outer pieced border: see diagrams. Then appliqué three red cherries in each square and one red cherry and two green leaves in each corner piece.

8. Make half-square triangle units. Join them to make the outer sawtooth border. Then sew to complete the quilt top.

Outer border

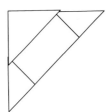

Make four.

Make four sets.

Step 6

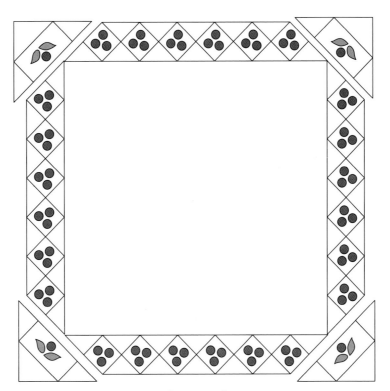

Placement of sets

Chapter 2

COLOR CHOICES

Color is the soul of a quilt. More than the geometric piecing or the appliquéd floral shape, it is the single choice that most conveys the maker's message and tells the story. Color is the vehicle used to express your intent, your flair, your memories, your sense of humor, and even the surprise of the happy accident. Because the colors we chose for our quilts reflect our own personalities, we have included a wide range of color choices representing other quilters. We want you to learn through experimenting how to trust your own feelings and preferences.

Who's afraid of selecting colors for a quilt? Almost everyone, and it's no wonder. You have just cut shapes from a beloved floral print. You adore this fabric, with its wide variety of leaves and blooms: it evokes your favorite season. You continue to cut other shapes in a variety of colors that co-ordinate with the print. You ponder, pleased with your color choices. You sew the shapes together, assemble the blocks, and view the results of your labors—with total disgust. The quilt is boring! What went wrong? Was the blue not right? Should it be green? You squint again and then get out your reducing glass. Oh! It must need another color, but what? You are confused.

It is difficult to recognize and identify the source of color errors. Because we all see color so differently and color choice is so intensely personal, what seems boring and insipid to one person appears delicate and subtle to someone else. Here are some ideas to help you avoid disappointment.

▶ COLOR CHOICES

Establish a Background Color

Background color affects your choices by interacting with the other colors. Some backgrounds recede, while others push forward. You can make some predictions through a quick trick: cut the shapes and lay them on various background colors, from dark to light, muted to bright. Let your eye interact with the colors in the background and then make your selection:

Did the colors recede from the background?

Can you distinguish the shapes, or did they disappear into the background?

Were the colors enhanced or subdued?

What background color set the stage to make *all* your color choices sing?

What background brought life and vitality to all the other colors?

All geometric blocks need a background pervading the quilt to set up the rhythm of the design. *Freddy's House* on page 55 has black and white fabrics around the house. Large motifs, as in *Star of Bethlehem* on page 86, can be broken up by letting the background color enter into the motif itself. This was done with the rows of dark diamonds placed so that the large motif can settle into the background. The use of the same background in the border is equally important; it lets the bright triangles flicker into and out of the border.

Push and Pull

When fabric is cut into shapes, its mood is altered as the fabric design is sliced into and only portions of the motif are visible. If the fabric design is large, with a lot of background color, the floral part will not be repeated very often, as in *Five Stripes* on page 18. Since the yellow floral is only occasionally seen, the viewer isn't even sure there are flowers.

Here are a few hints for cutting fabric design:

Start looking at fabric by the way it will cut into shapes. We like to give it the "cut-well" test. To do this, make a circle of an appropriate size with your finger and thumb on the surface of the fabric.

Large shapes preserve the mood and color of the original fabric, as in *Bow Tie* on page 43. The large shapes push forward and pull back, setting up a rhythm. The quilt retains the personality of the fabric: fun-loving, bold, full of bright energy. In the border the much smaller areas of color become grayed and subdued.

Do you know how to use the push and pull of warm and cool colors, advancing and receding? This is one of our favorite ways to keep colors active and alive. Think in terms of warm blue and cool blue, hot yellow and icy yellow. Beware of assumptions that all pinks are warm, because some appear frigid, just as some blue-greens appear warm—a far cry from the coolness of the dark blue of *Sailboat* on page 58. The warm and inviting blue-green surrounds the cool, stark sailboats. We have set up a positive-negative design trick. The eye doesn't know where to focus, because one background is dark and the other background is light; the sailboats push in and out. This gives the piece more interest and variety. *Sawtooth* on page 38 has many backgrounds, some warm and some cool, once more setting up the push and pull effect. The jewels in the *Jewel Box* quilts on page 130 are set in a granite-colored path, allowing the brilliant colors to vibrate in the foreground.

Allocating Color to the Individual Shapes

Selecting, rejecting, and varying your color choices for the individual shapes is an enjoyable part of the quiltmaking process. Select your background and allocate colors to the individual shapes, viewing carefully as the adjacent piece interacts. Decide what shapes you want the eye to identify; determine what shapes produce the desired pattern. You can identify this by laying the shapes on the background to see if there is enough contrast. Look at the shapes up close and at a distance. Then look with a reducing glass, always against the background colors. With a little distance between you and your work,

you will see the relative lightness and darkness (value).

Turn to page 35 and study Rosalee Sanders' *Basket* quilt. Each block has a different combination of backgrounds and shapes within the monochromatic family of cool red, mauve, pinks, maroon, and rose. Some blocks, almost indistinguishable from a distance, have low contrast. When the contrast is sharp and distinct, we can identify the basket. You can vary the effect, as Rosalee did, by setting up low, medium, and high contrast, adding excitement to the quilt. Use caution when working with a wide variety of fabrics to avoid setting up too much clutter. Allow the viewer's eye a resting point. Notice the dark, small diagonal sashing strips separating the blocks. This crisscross line unifies the colors and shapes. The sashing, posts, and border give a solid foundation and finish the composition.

Light Source

Light is the power. You should always seek the light shades in your pattern as your first priority. If the light source does not appear in your background area, it must highlight your shapes. Dark or grayed colors will showcase the brilliance of your lights. Mabry Benson's *Bar Quilt* on page 41 uses white and yellow. Mabry's *Lady of the Lake* on page 68 utilizes a variety of violets, ranging from light to dark, with red as an accent. Wherever the light source travels across the quilt, the viewer receives pleasant vibrations.

View each of the quilts in the book and identify the light source. Is it in the border, block patterns, or backgrounds? What important design elements are emphasized? Does the light travel, creating continuity? Does it set up a balance? Is it zigzag, diagonal, or just a small spark? Does it introduce a third dimension? This

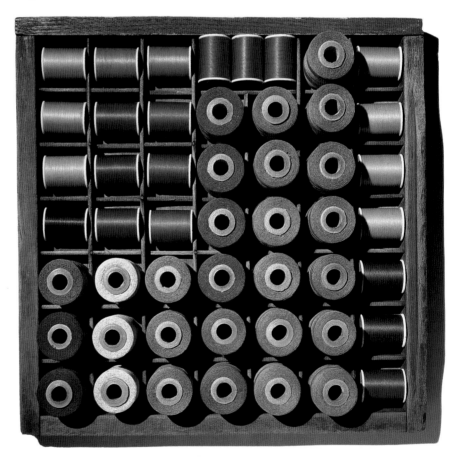

You can even look in your thread box for color and light inspiration.

exercise should lead you to new ways of color choices.

▶ COLOR INSPIRATION

We all need something tangible to see, study, and compare. Unless you copy precisely what you find in books and magazines, there must be another point of departure, some-place to start as you make your color choices. Following are some of the ways you can learn about using color—while also enjoying yourself.

Quilt Shows

We learn and are influenced by each other. How another person combines colors will help us develop our own style, enhanced by our familiarity with traditional or original designs. We suggest visiting a quilt show as you would visit a museum, for enjoyment but also for study.

1. Have an open mind to the color ideas of others. Let color mesmerize you; let it shock you.

2. Don't view each quilt you see with "I only like" in your mind. Blue and white may be your favorite combination, but force yourself to look closely at other combinations, appreciating something different.

3. View the show a second time, looking for something new. Make a mental note of your new discoveries.

4. Look slowly and carefully at each quilt, even if it doesn't appeal to you at first glance. View the quilt from a distance as well as up close.

5. Try to focus on details, designs, negative spaces, sizes, fabrics, and quilting lines. A quilt show is our favorite place to renew ourselves, to train the eye to see in depth.

Objects

Objects that we see and use each day in our homes tell a story of pleas-

More colors than you can count!

ure and discovery. These objects act as a constant personal source of inspiration. Blue and white china plates lined up on a stark white wall of Katie Prindle's dining room wall inspired a fabric collection in those colors, as well as another of fabrics with plate, cup, and saucer motifs. Our sampler quilt on page 106 reflects our color vision of many types and styles of china.

Traveling

If you are a fabric collector, you haunt shops and purchase fabrics from the special places you visit. *Treasured Hearts* (page 30) is made from Liberty of London fabrics that Diana purchased in Scotland and England. It may take several years to accumulate such a collection; however, if you let friends know you are collecting certain types, they will aid in your search and make the collection even more memorable.

Seasons

Nature suggests color ideas and provides us with unending combina-

tions. As each of us interprets and sees the seasons differently, we communicate our feelings in our quilts and in our fabric collections. When the delphiniums bloomed against the white picket fence, their stately blooms permeated our thoughts. Soon a bloom was picked and taken to the fabric shop to collect all the shades of periwinkle, cobalt, and other appropriate blues available. This collection of blues, plus the thoughts of delphiniums, sunny days, and Katie's plates inspired our sampler quilt on page 106. Our interpretation of Spring enters the *Four-Patch* quilt on page 12; its borders convey a link with nature. Sally Barlow's sampler on page 107 represents her interpretation of spring, with its growth and renewal.

Historical Styles

The fabrics of the 1930's are often reproduced and remain some of the most collectible fabric groups today. The small pastel prints give almost a faded or color-washed effect, reminiscent of another era. *Nine-Patch* on page 27 was made in 1930. However,

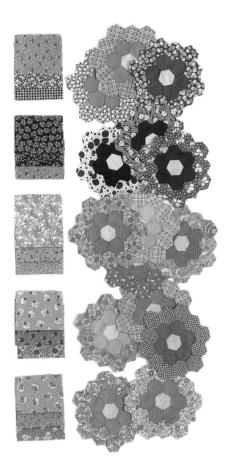

Above: Blocks from the 1930's and modern reproduction fabrics.
Below: Blocks from the nineteenth century and modern reproduction fabrics.

you can easily create a similar quilt with your own collection of thirties prints of ovals, dots, small flowers, and plaids.

Since so many of these fabrics are reproduced today, we can use double-pinks, indigos, madder prints, and turkey red as inspiration to imitate a nineteenth-century quilt.

Studying old quilts helps you to understand fabrics—how they have been used, and therefore how you can use them. We recommend that you read *Textile Designs* by Susan Meller and Joost Elffers, for further inspiration.

Fabric Collection

We suggest that you begin to build a fabric collection. The aim should be a variety of fabric designs and colors expressing your particular tastes and experiences. These fabrics are usually made into quilts, but some remain only as inspiration.

Several years ago, we started collecting conversational prints—fabrics picturing birds, fish, cats, dogs, etc. The fish fabric now became the theme and inspiration for *Sailboat.* Used in the pieced blocks and wide border, it highlights the theme fabric. Our friend Rosalee Sanders collects every blue-red undertoned printed fabric available, allowing her a wide selection for *Basket* on page 35.

Every quiltmaker will want to start a fabric collection of color families, to vary the color choices. Once you decide on a pattern for your quilt, this resource permits a large color selection. By varying one basic color in shade, tone, and intensity, and by varying the printed designs (dots, checks, other textures), your color families collection provides inspiration for the entire quilt. In *Courthouse Square* on page 79 you see a blending of colors within a color family: the building fronts contain many shades of red-dark, light, muted, and bright. Don't be afraid to use variety when you are working within one color family, for added depth and vitality.

Stripes and Plaids

Stripes and plaids serve as great additions because of their wonderfully versatile nature. They can create a contemporary, traditional, formal, or informal style, and they combine successfully with flowers as well as geometric prints. They provide a softening touch to break up the intricacies of patterns.

Sandy Klop's *Jewel Box,* on page 50, contains only fabrics of stripes, checks, and small figures, many collected from men's shirts. The posts provide a resting place for the eye and unify the varied plaids and stripes.

Group Quilts

When honoring someone on a special occasion, reflect the person's taste or home environment when choosing the colors to be used. *Brass Rings* on page 24 is a good example of a group of quilting friends saluting one of their circle. Each person brought a bright solid, reflecting Alice Johns' taste and her carousel horse collection. (Carousel fabric was used on the backing.) The choice of pattern also symbolizes the guild working and joining together in a common bond.

Another group of quilters brought a "starter" block in a bag. The center appliqué design, a folkart pattern, was completed several years ago by Claire Jarratt in an appliqué class. The center block set the pattern and color for the remaining borders, as shown in the *Folkart Medallion* quilt on page 94. The design, placed in the bag, was drawn by an anonymous recipient. This individual put on the first border. After completing her border, she placed her contribution into a bag. This procedure was repeated until the last person added the final border. The final border has red cherries that echo the center piece and the red zigzag of the first border. The blue side triangles give balance and finish the design, adding depth to the outer edge.

Furnishing Fabric

Because you have enjoyed large, romantic floral bouquets in your home, you might feel comfortable about using drapery fabric as a source of inspiration for a quilt. As you interpret the colors of the fabric, select eight or nine smaller-scale prints representing each of the leaves, ribbons, flowers, and backgrounds. Spread the fabrics out so you can see the placement of colors as you decide what to keep. Look again. Don't forget to consider all the colors you see in the drapery fabric, even if some are present in very small amounts. *Five Stripes* received its design and color inspiration from a drapery fabric.

EXERCISE:

1. Take a sufficiently large swatch of a drapery fabric.

2. *Look, see,* and *study* the colors and design.

3. Write down all the colors you see.

4. Write down all the details you see. Note the relative proportions of each color.

5. Label the background color or colors.

6. Choose eight or ten fabrics representing the color, mood, and style of each leaf and flower.

7. Spread the drapery fabric out and place each color on it, determining its value or intensity.

8. Decide which fabrics to keep.

9. Organize the "keepers," arranging the choices within each color family from light to dark.

10. Place all the color families together on a background.

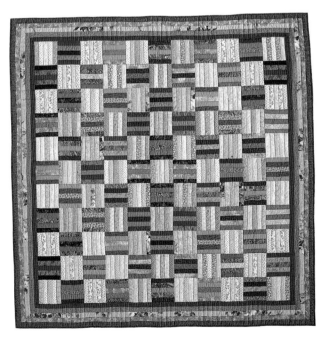

Furnishing fabric used for color inspiration for Five Stripes, *below.*

Chapter 3

SAMPLER QUILTS

A sampler is a medley of patterns combined to form a quilt. The patterns we have selected function as a model for the beginning student. They are intended to serve as references as you progress in learning quiltmaking. Since the patterns are given in sequence, easiest first, you will feel comfortable in completing each block.

The sampler was never intended to be an overwhelming project, but rather one in which, step by step, you can perfect the techniques required for each block, and with great accuracy. There is a lot of excitement as you work each block independently, choosing fabrics for the combinations. It is also fun and should never be taken too seriously. It is primarily a learning experience.

The sampler is valued as a good way to learn quiltmaking. It prepares students for long-term quilting: it offers a wide variety of blocks and construction techniques, setting blocks together, layering and basting, quilting and finally binding—the entire quiltmaking procedure. Years later, the student can look back to the first blocks and see the progression in skills, while also having the complete pleasure now of making an entire quilt.

As you view each of the samplers in this book, identify the block names and compare color choices. Find the *Album Patch* block in Katie's quilt and compare it with the one in the blue-and-white sampler and the one in Sally's quilt. As you study each of the samplers, note the various block settings, color balance, and especially the color choices that create a variety of moods.

This chapter contains a suggested class outline for making sampler quilts. Any of the 6″ and 12″ blocks in this book is appropriate for adding to a sampler quilt. You will find a line diagram of each of them, with cutting instructions for one single block. If you need help with construction, refer to the sew-order diagrams that accompany the pattern in Chapter 1.

▶ SAMPLER QUILT|CLASS— A SUGGESTED OUTLINE

▶SUPPLIES

- *Fabric: a variety of pieces (approximately 4 to 5 yards total in ¼ to ½ yard pieces)*

- *Tools: rotary cutter, cutting board, wide plastic ruler, fabric scissors, sewing machine, 100% cotton thread (neutral color), hand-sewing needle, glass-head pins, template plastic, ultra-fine permanent pen.*

Instructors demonstrate the techniques and block sew order during class. Students make the blocks they want to include in their quilt.

CLASS ONE: Quick-cutting and strip piecing techniques. Blocks: *Nine-Patch* and *Four-Patch*.

CLASS TWO: Half-square triangle technique. Blocks: *Sawtooth, Pieced Buttercup,* and *Jewel Box*.

CLASS THREE: Half-square triangles and double half-square triangles. Blocks: *Pine Trees, Sawtooth Star,* and *Sawtooth Star/Nine-Patch*.

CLASS FOUR: More double half-square triangles. Blocks: *Sailboat* and *Bow Tie* (6″ and 12″).

CLASS FIVE: More double half-square triangles. Blocks: *Martha Washington Star* and *Vestibule*.

CLASS SIX: Friendship blocks. Blocks: *Treasured Heart* and *Album Patch*.

CLASS SEVEN: Appliqué techniques. Blocks: *Apple Basket* and *Courthouse Square*.

CLASS EIGHT: Houses. Blocks: *Freddy's House* and *Row House*.

CLASS NINE: Settings and borders.

CLASS TEN: Layering and basting.

CLASS ELEVEN: Quilting and binding demonstration.

BLUE-AND-WHITE SAMPLER:

Sashing: Cut 1½″ wide strips
Posts: Cut 3½″ squares

SANDY'S SAMPLER:

Sashing: Cut 3½″-wide strips
Four-Patch posts: 3″ blocks
Cut 2″-wide strips
Inner and outer border:
Cut 1½″-wide strips
Middle border: Cut 2½″-wide strips

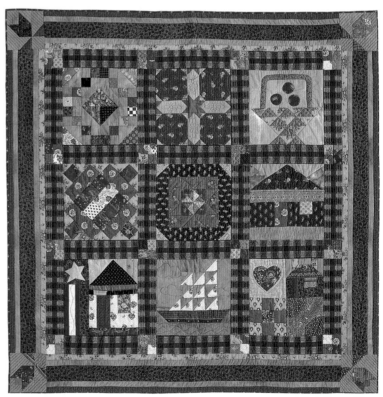

KATIE'S SAMPLER:

Sashing: Cut 2″-wide strips
Border: Cut 6″-wide strips

SALLY'S SAMPLER:

Inner and outer border:
Cut 2″-wide strips
Middle pieced border: Cut 2″ squares

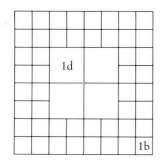

12" FOUR-PATCH BLOCK

(1b) forty-eight 2" squares, eight *each* of six fabrics

(1d) four 3½" squares

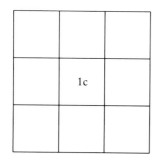

6" NINE-PATCH BLOCK

(1c) nine 2½" squares, four light and five dark *or* five light and four dark

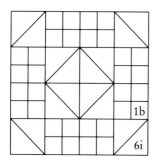

12" JEWEL BOX BLOCK

(1b) thirty-two 2" squares

(6i) eight 3⅞" squares *each* cut in half diagonally

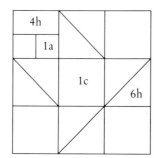

6" PIECED BUTTERCUP BLOCK

Background: (1a) one 1½" square

(1c) three 2½" squares

(4h) one 1½" x 2½" piece

(6h) two 2⅞" squares *each* cut in half diagonally

Flower center: (1a) one 1½" square

Flower: (6h) one 2⅞" square cut in half diagonally

(1c) one 2½" square

Leaves: (6h) one 2⅞" square cut in half diagonally

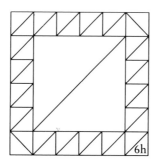

12" SAWTOOTH BLOCK

(6h) ten 2⅞" squares *each* light and dark. Cut squares in half diagonally.

Large triangles: two 8⅞" squares *each* cut in half diagonally. Use one triangle from each fabric.

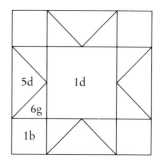

6" SAWTOOTH STAR BLOCK

(Block One of *Garden Maze* quilt pattern)

Background: (1b) four 2" squares

(5d) four 2" x 3½" pieces

Star: (1d) one 3½" square

(6g) eight 2" squares

Note: Cut sizes are for use with the double half-square triangle technique.

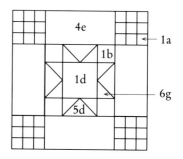

12" SAWTOOTH STAR/NINE-PATCH BLOCK

Sawtooth star:

Background: (1b) four 2" squares

(5d) four 2" x 3½" pieces

Star: (1d) one 3½" square

(6g) eight 2" squares

Note: Cut sizes are for use with the double half-square triangle technique.

Nine-Patches:

One 1½"-wide strip *each* light and dark

Use strip piecing technique. See *Nine-Patch* quilt for help.

(4e) four 3½" x 6½" pieces

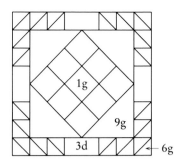

12" PINE TREES BLOCK

(1g) nine 2⅜" squares, five light and four dark

(3d) four 2" x 3½" pieces

(6g) ten 2⅜" squares *each* light and dark, cut in half diagonally

(9g) two 5⅜" squares *each* cut in half diagonally

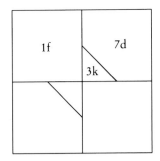

12" BOW TIE BLOCK

Background: (7d) two 6½" squares

Bow Tie: (1f) two 6½" squares

(3k) two 3½" squares

Note: Cut sizes are for use with the double half-square triangle technique.

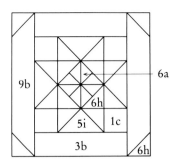

12" MARTHA WASHINGTON STAR BLOCK

(1c) four 2½" squares

(3b) two 2½" x 8½" pieces

(5i) four 2½" x 4½" pieces

(6a) four 2¼" squares *each* cut in half diagonally (2 light and 2 dark)

(6h) two 2⅞" squares *each* cut in half diagonally *and* twelve 2½" squares (eight star points and four corners)

(9b) two 2½" x 12½" pieces

Note: Cut sizes are for use with the double half-square triangle technique.

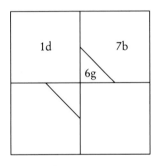

6" BOW TIE BLOCK

Background: (7b) two 3½" squares

Bow Tie: (1d) two 3½" squares

(6g) two 2" squares

Note: Cut sizes are for use with the double half-square triangle technique.

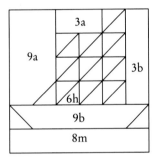

12" SAILBOAT BLOCK

Background: (3a) one 2½" x 4½" piece

(3b) one 2½" x 8½" piece

(6h) five 2⅞" squares *each* cut in half diagonally *and* two 2½" squares

(9a) one 4½" x 8½" piece

Sailboat: (6h) five 2⅞" squares *each* cut in half diagonally *and* one 2½" square

(9b) one 2½" x 12½" piece

Water: (8m) one 2½" x 12½" piece

Note: Cut sizes are for use with the double half-square triangle technique.

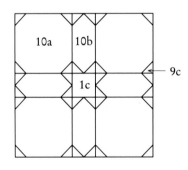

12" VESTIBULE BLOCK

(1c) one 2½" square

(9c) thirty-two 1½" squares (sixteen of color one and sixteen of color two)

(10a) four 5½" squares

(10b) four 2½" x 5½" pieces

Note: Cut sizes are for use with the double half-square triangle technique.

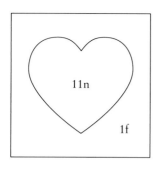

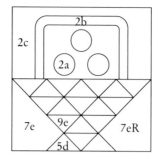

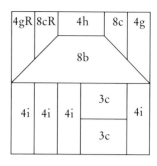

6″ TREASURED HEART BLOCK

(1f) one 6½″ square
(11n) one with template

12″ APPLE BASKET BLOCK

Background: (2c) one 6½″ x 12½″ piece
(7e) one and one reverse with template
(9e) three 3″ squares *each* cut in half diagonally
Apples: (2a) three with template
Handle: (2b) one with template
Basket: (9e) five 3″ squares *each* cut in half diagonally
Base: (5d) one 4¼″ square cut into quarters diagonally

6″ FREDDY'S HOUSE BLOCK

Window: (3c) one 2″ x 2½″ piece
House front: (3c) one 2″ x 2½″ piece
(4i) three 1½″ x 3½″ pieces
Door: (4i) one 1½″ x 3½″ piece
Sky: (4h) one 1½″ x 2½″ piece
(4g) one and one reverse with template
Roof: (8b) one with template
Chimneys: (8c) one and one reverse with template

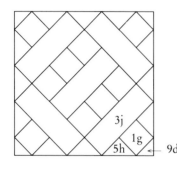

12″ ALBUM PATCH BLOCK

(1g) ten 2⅝″ squares
(3j) five 2⅝″ x 6⅞″ pieces
(5h) three 3⅛″ squares *each* cut into quarters diagonally
(9d) two 2⅝″ squares *each* cut in half diagonally
Trim edges to make a 12½″ block.

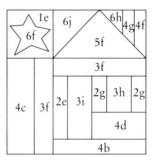

12″ COURTHOUSE SQUARE BLOCK

Flag: (1e) one 4½″ square
(3f) one 2″ x 8½″ piece
(4c) one 3″ x 8½″ piece
(6f) one with template
Sky: (4f, 6h and 6j) one 4⅞″ square cut in half diagonally
House: (2e) one 1¾″ x 5¾″ piece
(2g) two 1¾″ x 3½″ pieces
(3f) one 2″ x 8½″ piece
(3h) one 2⅝″ x 3½″ piece
(3i) one 2⅝″ x 5¾″ piece
(4b) one 1¾″ x 8½″ piece
(4d) one 2¾″ x 5⅛″ piece
(4g) one 1½″ x 3⅞″ piece
(5f) one with template

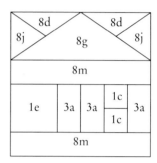

12″ ROW HOUSE BLOCK

Window: (1c) one 2½″ square
House front: (1c) one 2½″ square
(1e) one 4½″ square
(3a) two 2½″ x 4½″ pieces
Door: (3a) one 2½″ x 4½″ piece
Sky: (8d) two with template
Roof: (8g) one with template
Mountain: (8j) two with template
Eave and ground: (8m) one 2½″ x 12½″ piece *each*

Here is another sampler we made. Some of the blocks are different sizes, but this should give you some ideas for the different looks that are possible. The small blocks are each 5" (finished), and the large blocks are 8" (finished).

Chapter 4

TECHNIQUES

At this point you have selected a pattern, decided on the size of your quilt, and purchased the necessary fabric. In this chapter you will learn how to:

1. Prepare the fabric for cutting.

2. Cut the fabric into shapes, using quick or traditional techniques, or a combination of both.

3. Construct the quilt blocks.

All of the techniques you need to make any of the quilts in this book are included here. Some techniques may be very familiar to you, while others may be new. We have included practice exercises to help you become familiar with each technique while making a quilt block. We encourage you to work through these step-by-step instructions. The practice blocks can be incorporated into a sampler quilt. Samples and instructions for making four sampler quilts are included in Chapter 3. Supply lists are provided with each practice exercise so you can have everything ready. These exercises are helpful whether you are teaching yourself or learning in a class. If you are confident and want to skip the practice exercises, we strongly recommend that you make a practice block before cutting all the fabric. This will help you evaluate your color choices and technical skills.

There are certainly many useful techniques besides these. We have included those which work well for us in making the patterns in Chapter 1. We feel they are the easiest, most efficient, and most accurate for creating neat, flat pieced blocks. Although the quick methods are indeed quick, we caution you not to be tempted to compromise precision for the sake of speed. Accuracy is most important, every step of the way!

▶ PREPARING YOUR FABRIC

First you must prepare your fabric for cutting. You have three options: 1) pre-wash and pre-shrink; 2) pre-shrink only; or 3) do nothing. It is a good idea to remove any chemical treatments from fabrics that will be used to make a bed quilt, especially a baby quilt. However, wall quilts will resist mildew and fade less if the fabrics are not pre-treated. Read through the three options, evaluate how your quilt will ultimately be used, and then make your decision.

1. PRE-WASH AND PRE-SHRINK: This process will remove the chemicals from the fabrics and shrink them *before* the quilt is constructed. You can use a washing machine for this process. First, separate the lights from the darks. Then unfold them to a single thickness. Place the fabrics in

the washing machine in warm water. Use a laundry soap with a low pH, as detergents will pull color from the fabric. Run the fabric through a complete cycle. Using the instructions below, check to see if your washed fabric is colorfast. If it is, tumble dry until it is slightly damp. Press it and apply spray sizing to restore crispness, if you wish.

2. PRE-SHRINK: This process will only shrink the fabric but will *not* remove all of the chemicals. You can use a sink for this process. First, unfold the fabric to a single thickness. Place the fabric in warm (not hot), clear water. Add a 6″ square of white 100% cotton fabric. See if the fabric is releasing color into the water, or if the white fabric has changed color: if either has occurred, you will need to set the dye, following the instructions below. If there has been no color change, remove your fabric from the water and tumble dry until it is slightly damp. Press it and apply spray sizing to restore crispness if you wish.

3. DO NOTHING: Some quilters use the fabric exactly as it comes off the bolt, neither pre-washing nor pre-shrinking. You may choose only to test for colorfastness.

Check for Colorfastness
Regardless of which method of fabric preparation you choose, it is *always*

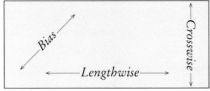

Selvage

Bias

Crosswise

Lengthwise

Selvage

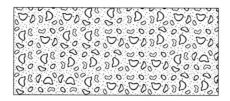

Non-directional print

Directional print

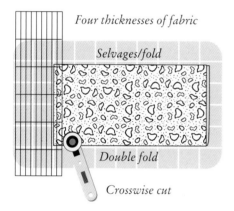

Four thicknesses of fabric

Selvages/fold

Double fold

Crosswise cut

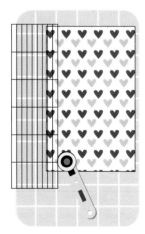

Single thickness of fabric

Lengthwise cut

Step 1

important to test for colorfastness, to prevent one color from bleeding into another when the quilt is washed for the first time. The fabrics to be very careful with are the deep red tones, teals, and purples. To test your fabric, cut a 2″ swatch. Then immerse the swatch into a clear glass of warm water. Check to see if there is any color change. If there is not, then you can proceed. If color is released and you have already pre-washed the fabric, then you must set the dye. If the fabric has not been pre-washed, then do so to remove the excess dye, following the instructions given above. Then re-test for color release in a clear glass of warm water. If the water still changes color, then set the dye.

Setting the Dye

This process has been successful in setting the dye in some fabrics. If it does not work, *do not* use the fabric in your quilt. To set the dye, soak the fabric in *undiluted* white vinegar. Use approximately one gallon of white vinegar for three yards of fabric. Rinse the fabric thoroughly two to three times in clear, warm water, then re-test a swatch in a glass of warm water. If there is no color change, dry the fabric completely, then press it. Apply spray sizing if desired to restore crispness.

▶ QUICK-CUTTING

"Quick-cutting" describes the time-saving methods of cutting fabric shapes using a rotary cutter, cutting

board, and wide plastic ruler. These tools were introduced in the early 1980's and allowed quilters to cut multiple layers of fabrics quickly and accurately into a variety of shapes.
 WARNING: It is important to use the same cutting tools throughout your project, as markings on rulers and cutting boards can vary slightly, resulting in finished blocks of different sizes. Cut fabric strips along the crosswise grain (from selvage to selvage), as yardage for the quilts is based on crosswise cuts. Most cotton fabrics vary in width from 42″ to 48″. For the purposes of this book, the crosswise width of the fabric is assumed to be 42″.

It is important that the crosswise strips be straight. To prevent bent strips, first press the fabric flat to eliminate the crease created when it was folded on the bolt. Then fold your piece of fabric in half lengthwise, with the right side facing you and the selvages even with each other. The folded edge should be without ripples. If it does ripple, hold the folded fabric and slide one selvage edge to the right or left until the folded edge is smooth.

One of the many advantages of using quick-cutting tools is the ability to cut through several thicknesses of fabric. You can easily cut up to four thicknesses if you are working with a solid color or non-directional print fabric. However, when you cut fabric with lengthwise stripes, plaids, or directional prints, the results are more pleasing if your strips are cut following the lengthwise grain, cutting only one thickness at a time.

Quick-Cutting Strips

Refer to the diagrams for help in determining the best direction and number of thicknesses for cutting your fabric. Then cut strips, as follows. Note: Instructions are for right-handed people; left-handed people should reverse the placement.

✂ *HELPFUL HINT*: There are several brands of rotary cutters available. We recommend the one with the larger wheel. It is well worth the investment, as the results are much better. Replacement blades are available but, unless you are convinced your blade is old or damaged, sometimes it needs only a little cleaning and a bit of oil to make it run smoothly again. When replacing the blade, carefully remove all parts and reassemble them in the exact reverse order to avoid mistakes.

☞ *WARNING*: Rotary-cutter blades are very sharp; be careful during use, and always keep the safety lock on when the cutter is not being used. Do not leave it around for small hands to explore: it can be a hazard.

1. Lay your fabric on the cutting board. If you are cutting multiple layers, first fold the fabric to four thicknesses. Then use your wide plastic ruler and rotary cutter to straighten the left-hand edge.

If you are cutting a single thickness along the lengthwise grain, use the wide plastic ruler and rotary cutter to remove the selvage.

2. Place the marking for the width of the strip even with the newly cut edge of the fabric. Then use the rotary cutter to cut off a strip of fabric.

3. Continue cutting strips the required width for the pattern you have selected.

Quick-Cutting Shapes from Strips

Once you have cut fabric strips, you can then cut those strips into many other shapes for pieced quilt block patterns. *Always remember to include ¼″ seam allowance when cutting the fabric strips.*

SQUARES

Cut strips the desired width. Then cut the strips apart to make squares. For example, to cut 2″ squares, cut a 2″-wide strip of fabric. Then cut the strip apart every 2″ to make squares.

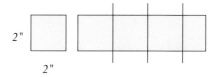

RECTANGLES

Cut strips the desired length. Then cut the strips apart the necessary width to make rectangles. For example, to cut 2″ x 4″ rectangles, cut a 4″-wide strip of fabric. Then cut the strip apart every 2″ to make 2″ x 4″ rectangles.

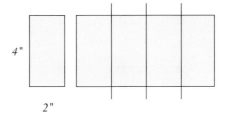

TRIANGLES

The direction of the grainline determines the cut size of the strips to make the triangles. ✂ *HELPFUL HINT*: Look at the template patterns found at the back of the book. The grainline, indicated by the arrow, is marked on each pattern. If you are unsure of the *cut* size of a shape, measure the solid line of the appropriate side on the template pattern. If you are unsure of the *finished* size of a shape, measure the length of the broken line.

To quick-cut these triangles, you must know the *finished* size of side X. Add ⅞″ to this measurement to determine the *cut* size of the fabric strip. For example, to cut a triangle with a finished size of 2″ on side X, cut a 2⅞″ wide strip. Cut the strip into 2⅞″ squares. Then cut the squares in half diagonally to make triangles. Since

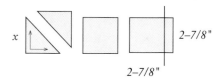

you are cutting multiple layers, be very careful to cut accurately from corner to corner when cutting diagonally across the squares. Do not let underlying layers slip.

To quick-cut these triangles, you must know the *finished* size of side X. Add 1¼″ to this measurement to determine the *cut* size of the fabric strip. For example, to cut a triangle with a finished size of 3″ on side X, cut a 4¼″ wide strip. Cut the strip into 4¼″ squares. Then cut the squares into quarters diagonally. Since you are cutting multiple layers, be very careful to cut accurately from corner to corner when cutting diagonally across the squares. Do not let underlying layers slip.

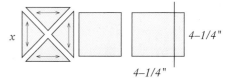

The following shapes incorporate quick-cutting with plastic templates. Refer to the section on "Making Plastic Templates" for help if necessary.

To quick-cut these triangles, you must measure the template pattern in the back of the book to determine the distance, as indicated by the arrow in the diagram. Then cut strips this measurement. Lay the plastic template on the fabric strip and use a marking pencil to mark the correct angle. Then use the cutting tools to cut the triangles apart, as shown in the diagram.

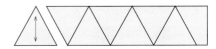

60° triangle for Six-Pointed Star Variation

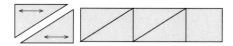

Triangle used for sky in Row House block

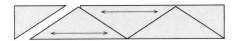

Triangle used for roof in Row House block

This same method of cutting fabric strips and using plastic templates to mark the angle is also useful for other patterns in this book.

▶ TRADITIONAL CUTTING

Some quilters are not comfortable with quick-cutting techniques and prefer to use traditional methods. We have included, at the back of the book, template patterns for all of the shapes needed for the quilt blocks. The inner broken line indicates the *finished* size of the shape. This is also the stitching line. The outer solid line indicates the *cut* size, including the seam allowance. Plastic templates can be made from these patterns. There is a line drawing of the pattern you selected in Chapter 1 that indicates the template patterns required for making it. Some template patterns are grouped together. Be careful to use only those lines required for your pattern.

There are two schools of thought about making templates for traditional cutting. Some quilters prefer to

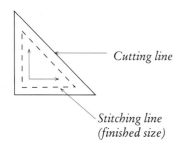

Cutting line

Stitching line (finished size)

make a plastic template of the *finished* size of the shape. This shape is then marked onto the wrong side of the fabric and then the shape is cut ¼″ from the marked lines. Others prefer to make a template of the *cut* size of the shape. This shape is then marked onto the wrong side of the fabric and cut out. The line of stitching is then marked ¼″ in from the cut edges. Either method works equally well.

Making Plastic Templates

1. Lay a piece of template plastic over the desired template pattern in the back of the book.

2. With a fine-line permanent pen and large transparent ruler, mark directly over the lines.

3. Use a rotary cutter, wide plastic ruler, and cutting board, or a pair of paper scissors, to cut the template out, cutting just *inside* the line.

4. Use the permanent pen to write on the template: pattern name, template number, block size, and direction of grainline. ✄ *HELPFUL HINT*: Some template patterns, such as the roof on the *Row House*, contain large black dots along the stitching line. This dot is helpful for matching and joining shapes correctly. It must be transferred onto the wrong side of the fabric shape. To do this, first mark the dot onto the plastic template. Then pierce the dot with a thick needle or pin to create a hole. Place the plastic template over the wrong side of the fabric shape, insert the tip of a marking pencil into the hole, and mark the dot.

Cutting Fabric Shapes Using Templates

Now that you have made a plastic template, cut the shape from your fabric.

1. With the wrong side facing up, place a single thickness of fabric on a flat surface. Lay the plastic template on top of the fabric, making sure the grainline marking on the template

corresponds with the fabric.

2. Using a marking pencil (light-colored for dark fabrics), mark around the template. ✄ *HELPFUL HINT*: If you are using a *non-directional* fabric, you can cut up to four thicknesses at once. Make sure the fabric is smooth and the selvages are evenly matched. Keep the folds aligned with either light pressing or a few pins. If your fabric is *directional*, cut a single thickness at a time.

3. For a single layer of fabric, make long, cutting strokes with very sharp scissors. To cut multiple thicknesses with scissors, pin the fabrics together inside the marked lines to keep them from slipping.

▶ PREPARATION FOR SEWING

Now that you have cut out your individual fabric shapes, you are ready to join them into units and begin constructing the quilt block. Sewing (sometimes called piecing) can be done by either machine or hand.

In quiltmaking, we always use a ¼″ seam allowance—the distance from the cut edge of the fabric to the line of stitching. *Unless otherwise indicated, we will be using ¼″ seam allowances throughout this book.*

An accurate ¼″ seam allowance is important to the success of your pieced blocks. If you are using a sewing machine you must determine the correct placement of the fabric as it travels under the presser foot. Some machines have ¼″ guidelines marked on the throat plate; other machines have adjustable needle positions, allowing you to move the needle and use the edge of the presser foot as a guide. Whichever your situation, take time to make a sample and learn to make an accurate ¼″ seam with your machine.

If you are hand piecing, you can use a small transparent ruler and marking pencil (light-colored for dark fabrics) to mark the stitching line on the wrong side of every fabric shape. The stitching line is ¼″ in from the cut edge of the shape. Do not mark into the seam allowances.

▶ MACHINE PIECING

Nothing is more frustrating than sewing on a machine that skips stitches or becomes jammed. Take a few minutes to see that your machine is running smoothly, making even stitches on both the top and underside. Insert a new needle (No. 10 or 12 Universal) and remove any lint from the bobbin area. Unless you are working on very dark fabric, a neutral color 100% cotton thread works well for sewing the shapes together. Use the same thread in the top and the bobbin.

Organize your workspace and lay out the fabric shapes to be sewn. This will not only save time but can also prevent sewing errors.

1. Pick up two fabric shapes and place them right sides facing. Put them under the presser foot and sew them together along their right-hand edges. Do not backstitch.

2. To save time and thread, sew another pair of shapes together right behind the first pair. This is called chaining.

3. Continue sewing remaining shapes together.

4. Press the pieced shapes. Then cut the chain of threads holding them together. Refer to the section on "Pressing" for help.

▶ HAND PIECING

Many quilters enjoy the relaxing time spent in hand piecing. Although it is more time-consuming than machine piecing, it is certainly convenient if you want to do some piecing during lunch hour or while waiting in a doctor's office. You may want to try making one of the blocks using this method: it may turn you into a hand piecer.

Use a small needle (No. 10 Betweens) and an 18″ length of quilting thread; a neutral color is good. Do not knot the end of the thread.

1. With their right sides facing, place two fabric shapes together. Secure them with pins.

2. Insert the needle at the beginning of the marked line and make two small backstitches, leaving a 1″ tail.

3. Continue stitching across the marked line with small running stitches. Keep your stitches small, even, and not too tight. Check to see that the stitches go through the marked lines on both the front and back shapes.

4. To finish joining the two shapes, make two small backstitches at the end of the marked line. *Never stitch into the seam allowance.* Cut the thread, leaving a 1″ tail.

5. Press the pieced shapes.

▶ PRESSING

Pressing is an important part of quiltmaking. Get in the habit of pressing often as you sew, because it can determine the success or failure of block construction.

Set your steam iron on the cotton setting. Use a well-padded pressing surface, such as an ironing board covered with a light-colored towel. The padding prevents the seam allowance from creating a ridge on the right side of the pieced block.

With the darker shape facing you, lay the shapes on the pressing surface and press the seam flat on the wrong side. Then fold the darker shape back over the stitching line and press. The seam will be turned in the direction of the darker fabric and prevent shad-

Machine piecing

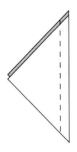

Step 1

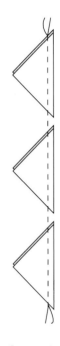

Steps 2–3

Hand piecing

Start and stop 1/4″ from edge.

Steps 2–4

owing under the lighter fabric. To avoid possible distortion, allow the fabrics to cool before moving them from the pressing surface.

It is not always possible to press seams in the direction of the darker fabric. Some units with several seams will have a mind of their own. If this is the case, it is best to comply and press in the direction they wish to go. The block will lie flatter if you do.

▶ STRIP PIECING

Many of the patterns in this book can be made using the time-saving methods of strip piecing. Fabric strips

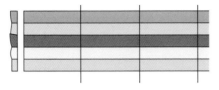

Strip piecing

are sewn together on the sewing machine in desired combinations. The sewn strips are then cut apart to make new shapes. The width of the cut strips is determined by the individual quilt pattern.

1. Lay two fabric strips right sides facing and sew them together side by side. Be very careful not to pull or stretch the strips while sewing, so

they do not become wavy.

2. Sew on any remaining strips in the proper sequence. Press the strips. Allow them to cool before moving.

✂ *HELPFUL HINT*: To avoid rippling when you sew several strips together into units, trim all the strips to the same length before sewing. Then sew the strips together side by side. This is especially helpful if fabric weights vary slightly.

3. Place the cooled strips on the cutting board with their right sides facing up. First cut one short end straight, using the rotary cutter and wide plastic ruler. Then cut pieces to the width indicated by your quilt pattern.

PRACTICE EXERCISE: STRIP PIECING

Four-Patch

▶ SUPPLIES:
- *Fabric: Three 2" x 17" pieces of light fabric, three 2" x 17" pieces of dark fabric, and four 3½" squares (2 light and 2 dark)*
- *Rotary cutter*
- *Wide plastic ruler*
- *Cutting board*
- *Sewing machine*
- *100% cotton thread (neutral)*
- *Glass-head pins*
- *Steam iron*
- *Pressing surface*
- *Light-colored towel*

1. Sew the 2" x 17" pieces together into three sets of light and dark, as shown.

2. Cut the sets apart every 2", as shown.

3. Sew the cut strips together to make four-patch blocks. There should be four each of three combinations (twelve blocks).

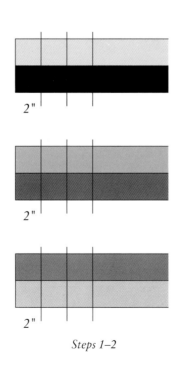

Steps 1–2

4. Lay out all the units and sew them together in rows, as shown.

5. Join rows together to make a complete block. It should measure 12½". Give it a final press.

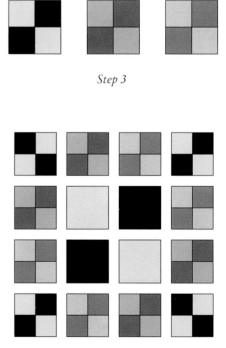

Step 3

Step 4

118
▼

▶ HALF-SQUARE TRIANGLES

These units are made by joining two right-angle triangles along their longer sides. They are found in many pieced quilt block patterns. There are many quick methods for making them, and we have included one that we like.

1. Place the two fabrics to be used right sides facing. Since fabric widths vary, you may only be able to line two selvages with each other.

2. Be sure the layered fabrics are smooth, then fold to four thicknesses.

3. Straighten the left-hand edges and cut the desired strip width. Refer to the section on "Quick-Cutting" for help. The width of the strips is ⅞″ larger than the *finished* size of the unit.

4. Cut the strips to make squares, then cut the squares in half diagonally to make triangles. It is important to

cut accurately from corner to corner. Do not let underlying layers slip. The triangles are conveniently arranged alternately, right sides together and ready for sewing.

5. Sew the triangles together in pairs, chaining one pair directly after the other, as shown.

6. Lay the units with the darker side facing up and press first on the wrong side. Then fold the darker triangle back over the stitching line and press to form a square. Cut the threads holding the pairs together.

7. Trim the two extensions, as shown, to complete the unit.

▶ DOUBLE HALF-SQUARE TRIANGLES

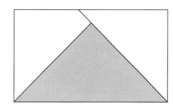

Double half-square triangles are units of three triangles, as shown. We like this method of constructing the unit, as it does not involve cutting any

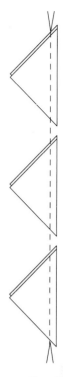

Step 5

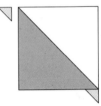

Step 7

PRACTICE EXERCISE: HALF-SQUARE TRIANGLES

Pine Trees

▶SUPPLIES:
- ¼ yard light-colored cotton fabric
- ¼ yard dark cotton fabric
- Rotary cutter
- Cutting board
- Fabric scissors
- Glass-head pins
- 100% cotton thread (neutral)
- Sewing machine
- Steam iron
- Pressing surface
- Light-colored towel

1. Cut:
- Five 2⅜″ squares of light-colored fabric
- Four 2″ x 3½″ rectangles of light-colored fabric
- Four 2⅜″ squares of dark fabric
- Two 5⅜″ squares of dark fabric. Cut each square in half diagonally.
- Quick-cutting: ten 2⅜″ squares *each* of light and dark

2. Make the half-square triangle units.

3. To complete the block, proceed to the practice exercise for Unit Construction on page 122.

triangles, only squares and rectangles. This makes cutting easier for the beginner and keeps the finished unit straight. Note that these are general instructions and no sizes are given. Refer to the pattern you are making for specific cutting measurements.

1. Place a square on top of a rectangle, with their right sides facing. Then stitch through both thicknesses diagonally, as shown. Be very careful to stitch from corner to corner in order to keep the angle sharp. ✄ *HELPFUL HINT*: Finger press or use an iron to press a diagonal crease lightly in the square, as a guideline for

stitching, or use a marking pencil to mark the angle.

2. Press the top layer of fabric (the square) back over the stitching line. Check to see that its two edges are in line with the edges of the rectangle. If they do not line up exactly, your stitching line is not accurate.

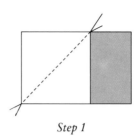

Step 1

3. With their right sides facing, place another square on top of this unit. Then stitch across it diagonally, as shown. ✄ *HELPFUL HINT*: If you are using a directional printed fabric such as a stripe, lay it on the rectangle with the stripes facing the same direction, so that the finished unit

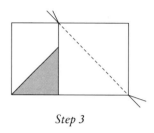

Step 3

PRACTICE EXERCISE: DOUBLE HALF-SQUARE TRIANGLES

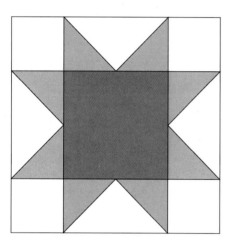

Sawtooth Star

▶ SUPPLIES:
- *⅛ yard each of two cotton fabrics (one light and one dark)*
- *Rotary cutter or fabric scissors*
- *Wide plastic ruler*
- *Cutting board*
- *Sewing machine*
- *100% cotton thread (neutral)*
- *Glass-head pins*
- *Fabric scissors*
- *Steam iron*
- *Pressing surface*
- *Light-colored towel*

1. Using traditional or quick-cutting techniques, cut:
- Four 2″ x 3½″ rectangles of light fabric

- Four 2″ squares of light fabric
- One 3½″ square of dark fabric
- Eight 2″ squares of dark fabric

2. Following the general instructions above, sew the 2″ squares of dark fabric to the light rectangles to make double half-square triangle units.

3. Lay the shapes as shown in the diagram.

4. Lay the shapes from Row 2 right sides together with the shapes in Row 1. Then stitch together along their right-hand edges, as shown. Do not cut the chain of thread connecting the units.

✄ *HELPFUL HINT*: Stitch just to the right of the point where the stitching lines cross on the double half-square triangle unit, to avoid cutting off the point on the right side.

5. Turn the unit 180°. Lay the remaining shapes as shown. Then stitch them, right sides together, with the shapes in Row 1. Stitch as in Step 4. Do not cut the chain of thread connecting the units.

6. Press the seams in the direction of the squares (top and bottom rows, press out; middle row, press in).

7. Fold the top row toward the middle row and stitch. Repeat for the bottom row.

8. The block is complete and should measure 6½″. Give it a final press.

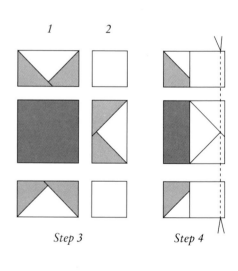

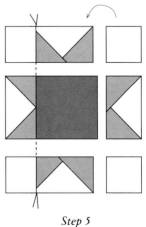

Step 5

▼

will have stripes running in the same direction, as shown.

4. Press the square fabric back over the stitching line. Turn the unit to the wrong side. Check to see that all the edges of the squares and rectangles are even with each other. If just a bit of the square fabric extends beyond the edges of the rectangle, simply trim it even. The rectangle is your guide for an accurate finished unit.

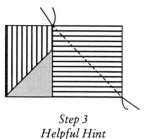

Step 3
Helpful Hint

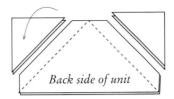

Cut back two layers ONLY.

Back side of unit

Step 5

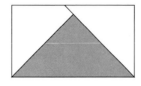

Step 5
Finished

5. Trim off the excess fabric (cut the two layers of fabric behind the triangles) to within ¼″ of the stitching lines, as shown. Give the unit a final press.

▶ BONUS HALF-SQUARE TRIANGLES

If you are concerned with the waste that results from making double half-square triangles, here is a helpful hint for you. When the units are small, the waste is minimal. However, as the size of the unit increases, the amount of waste can add up.

1. Complete Step 1 of "Double Half-Square Triangles."

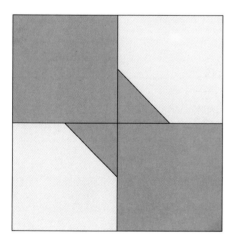

Bow Tie

▶ SUPPLIES:
• *¼ yard of cotton fabric for bow tie*
• *¼ yard of cotton fabric for background*
• *Rotary cutter*
• *Cutting board*
• *Wide plastic ruler*
• *Fabric scissors*
• *Glass-head pins*
• *100% cotton thread (neutral)*
• *Sewing machine*
• *Steam iron*
• *Pressing surface*
• *Light-colored towel*

1. Using quick or traditional cutting techniques, cut:
• Two 6½″ squares of bow tie fabric
• Two 3½″ squares of bow tie fabric
• Two 6½″ squares of background fabric

2. With their right sides facing, sew each 3½″ square of bow tie fabric to each 6½″ square of background fabric. Sew the shapes together, stitching diagonally from corner to corner, as shown.

3. Run another row of stitching ⅜″ to ½″ away from the first line of stitching, as shown.

4. Fold the triangle of bow tie fabric over the stitching lines and press.

5. Use your fabric scissors to cut between the stitching lines, as shown.

6. Press the two cut pieces open to make half-square triangle units. Set them aside.

7. For the block sew order, see the diagram.

8. Your block is complete and should measure 12½″. Give it a final press.

9. The two bonus half-square triangle units can begin a collection for your future projects.

Step 3

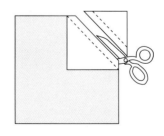

Step 5

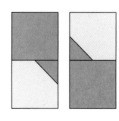

Step 7

2. Run another stitching line ⅜″ to ½″ away from the first line of stitching, as shown.

3. Complete Steps 2 and 3 of "Double Half-Square Triangles."

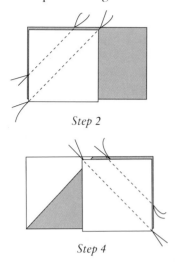
Step 2

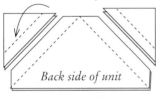
Step 4

Cut back two layers ONLY.

Back side of unit
Step 5

4. Run another stitching line ⅜″ to ½″ away from the first line of stitching, as shown.

5. Trim the excess fabric (two layers of fabric behind the triangles) *between* the stitching lines, as shown. It is all right if the seams are slightly less than ¼″.

Each double half-square triangle unit will give two bonus half-square triangle units. You will have to check these half-square triangle units for accuracy and trim them to a uniform size before incorporating them into a quilt block or pieced border, as we did on the border of the *Bow Tie* quilt.

▶ UNIT CONSTRUCTION

Organizing your fabric shapes for sewing is important for successful block construction. Individual shapes are joined to make units, and then units are joined to make a completed block. Not only is this a time-saving technique but it is also helpful in pre-

venting shapes from inadvertently being turned the wrong way during sewing.

1. Arrange all of the shapes on a flat surface in the proper order for the pieced block. Then sew shapes (squares, rectangles, triangles, etc.) or units (half-square triangles or double half-square triangles) together in pairs. Sew all of the pairs required for the block or quilt you are making at one time. Chain all of the pairs one after the other to save time and thread.

2. Cut the chain of thread connecting the new units. Continue sewing as many units as the block requires.

3. Read through the practice exercise below, applying this method to the *Pine Trees* quilt block.

▶ SEW ORDER

Block sew order is the sequence in which shapes or units of shapes are best sewn together to produce neat, accurate pieced quilt blocks. Sug-

Pine Trees

▶ SUPPLIES:
- *Fabric shapes cut for the* Pine Trees *block as instructed in the Practice Exercise on page 119*
- *Sewing machine*

- *100% cotton thread (neutral)*
- *Glass-head pins*
- *Steam iron*
- *Pressing surface*
- *Light-colored towel*

1. Arrange and then sew the nine 2⅝″ squares, as shown.

✄ *HELPFUL HINT*: If an entire quilt is made from this pattern, it is easier and more efficient to use strip-piecing methods for making this nine-patch unit, rather than cutting individual squares.

2. For unit construction, see the diagrams.

(You will complete this block in the next Practice Exercise.)

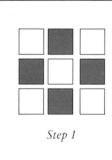
Step 1

Make four units.   *Make four units.*

Make four units.

Make two units.
Step 2

gested sew order diagrams are given with each of the quilt patterns in this book. Study them carefully before beginning to sew. Following is a practice exercise for completing the *Pine Trees* quilt block, to help you become familiar with sew order diagrams.

▶ APPLIQUÉ

Appliqué is one method of quiltmaking that allows a quilter free rein to apply decoration to the background fabric. This method of letting creative impulses enter your work is the spice and pleasure that people throughout history have enjoyed; they embellish cloth with realistic and stylized designs representing leaves, flowers, hearts, birds, plants, animals, symbols, portraits, and even life histories and events. The designs are limitless. This need to decorate cloth has certainly entered into our quiltmaking skills, and we chose several patterns on a beginning level so you can experiment with making circles, curves, inverted points, and sharp points. The appliqué motifs are all folkloric: star (*Courthouse Square*), heart (*Treasured Hearts*), apples and handles (*Apple Basket*), and birds, tree, and leaves (*Folkart Medallion*).

The problem which often arises in appliqué is how to deal with the turn-under allowance and eliminate bulk in order to produce neat, flat motifs with smooth edges. Included in this section are three methods of preparing your motif for either hand or machine appliqué. We encourage you to try all of them with the *Treasured Heart* block in the practice exercise, found at the end of the chapter.

Method One: Paper-Basting

Here is one method we have used a lot and still think it is one of the most accurate.

1. Carefully trace the motif from the template pattern in the back of the book onto a plain piece of paper. You will need one paper pattern for each shape in the design: twenty leaves, fifteen cherries, etc. For those shapes that are not symmetrical (the turkey in *Folkart Medallion*, for example), mark an X on the paper to indicate its right side.

2. Cut out the individual shapes with your paper scissors.

3. Lay the paper patterns right side down onto the wrong side of the fabric. Pin to secure.

4. Hand baste. Then remove the pins.

5. Cut out the fabric shape ¼″ larger than the paper pattern all the way around. Turn the ¼″ allowance to the wrong side and baste around the edges. Press the shape.

Basting varies slightly from shape to shape. Here are a few hints for ease in basting:

Pine Trees

▶ SUPPLIES:
• *Fabric shapes and units for the* Pine Trees *quilt block*
• *Sewing machine*
• *100% cotton thread (neutral)*
• *Glass-head pins*
• *Steam iron*
• *Pressing surface*
• *Light-colored towel*

1. Sew the fabric shapes and units together to complete the *Pine Trees* quilt block, following the diagrams below.

2. The block is complete and should measure 12½″. Give it a final press.

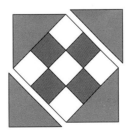

123
▼

Hearts

HEARTS: Make a small clip at the V, just shy of the paper pattern. With the knot on the front side, begin the basting stitches on a curved side. Fold the allowance to the wrong side and take basting stitches around the edges, spreading the fabric apart at the V. Continue stitching around the heart, up to the point, then folding the allowance on the opposite side to the wrong side. Continue basting. Press the shape.

LEAVES: With the knot on the right side, begin the basting stitches on a curved side. Stitch up to the point, then fold the seam allowance from the opposite side to the wrong side and continue stitching. Repeat for the opposite point. Do not cut off the fabric extensions at the points. They will be tucked under when the leaf is sewn to the background fabric. Press the shape.

6. Place the basted shapes onto the right side of the background fabric. ✂ *HELPFUL HINT*: For designs that have many motifs, such as the *Folkart Medallion*, it is helpful to make a photocopy of the overall design first.

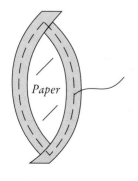

Leaves
Paper basting method

Then place the background fabric over the design and lightly mark the position of each shape.

7. Pin and then baste the shapes in place. Remove the pins.

8. Stitch the shapes to the background fabric using a small back whipstitch, stopping ½″ from the starting point on the motif. Refer to the following section on "Hand Appliqué" for help with the back whipstitch.

9. Remove the basting stitches and then the paper pattern. Use a pair of tweezers if necessary.

10. Sew the opening. Then end with two small stitches on the wrong side. ✂ *HELPFUL HINT*: On larger motifs such as the heart, stitch all the way around the motif. Cut away the background fabric underneath the motif to within ¼″ of the stitching line. Then remove the paper pattern.

11. Give the block a final press.

Method Two: Needle Turn with Freezer Paper

Freezer paper pressed to the right side of each motif acts as a guideline for turning under the allowance. Use plastic-coated freezer paper that can be purchased at your local grocery store.

1. With the rough side facing you, lay a piece of freezer paper over the template pattern. Use an ultra-fine permanent pen to trace the motif onto the paper. ✂ *HELPFUL HINT*: Trace the required number of shapes for the overall design.

2. Use your paper scissors to cut the shapes, cutting just inside the line.

3. With the right side facing up, place a single thickness of fabric on the pressing surface. With the rough side down, place the paper patterns on the fabric. Leave at least ½″ between the shapes for ease in cutting.

4. Use a steam iron to press the paper shapes to the fabric, pressing firmly and carefully to avoid ripples.

5. With your fabric scissors, cut the shapes apart ⅛″ beyond the edges of the pattern.

6. With the paper side face up, place the cut shape onto the background in the desired position.

7. Pin, then hand baste the fabric shapes into position. Do not allow the basting stitches to get closer than ¼″ from the edges, as you may need room for clipping curves or V's and turning under a ⅛″ allowance. Remove the pins.

Clipping varies from shape to shape. Here are a few hints:

V's: Make a small clip into the allowance, stopping just short of the

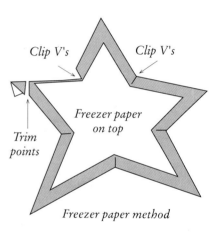

Freezer paper method

Points: Cut excess fabric approximately ⅛″ beyond the point. The allowance is turned and stitched on one side, up to the point. Then the allowance from the opposite side is tucked under and stitched.

8. Thread your No. 10 Betweens needle with a single strand of thread in a color to match the motif. Secure one end with a knot.

9. Use the tip of your needle to turn the edges of the motif under ⅛″, using the edge of the freezer paper as a guide. Hold it in place with the thumb of your free hand. ✂ *HELPFUL HINT*: The tip end of your embroidery scissors is helpful in turning under those areas that are difficult to turn with the needle.

10. Using a small back whipstitch, appliqué the motifs to the background fabric. Refer to the following "Hand Appliqué" section for help with the back whipstitch.

✂ *HELPFUL HINT*: Work approximately ½" to 1" ahead of the stitches in turning the allowance with the tip of your needle.

11. Remove the basting stitches. Then carefully peel off the freezer paper pattern from the front side.

12. Give the completed block a final press.

Method Three: Spray Starch

This method works extremely well on many motifs such as hearts, circles, stars, and leaves. It is appropriate with either hand or machine appliqué.

1. Lay a piece of template plastic over the pattern and use an ultra-fine permanent pen to trace the motif onto the plastic.

2. Use your paper scissors to cut the plastic template out, cutting just inside the line.

3. Lay the plastic template on top of a manila file folder. Using an ultra-fine permanent pen, mark around the template.

4. Use your paper scissors to cut the cardboard template, cutting just inside the line. ✂ *HELPFUL HINT*: It is necessary to make only one cardboard template for each different motif, as it is reusable.

5. With the wrong side up, place a single thickness of fabric on a flat surface. Lay the cardboard pattern on top

Circles
Spray starch method

of the fabric. Using a marking pencil (light-colored for dark fabrics), mark around the motif, ¼" larger than the cardboard template.

6. Using fabric scissors, cut the fabric out, cutting on the marked line.

7. With the wrong side up, place the fabric motif on the pressing surface. Center the cardboard template over the fabric motif.

✂ *HELPFUL HINT*: To achieve a smooth curve around a circle, first run a small basting stitch around the edge of the fabric shape to distribute the fullness evenly. Center the cardboard circle onto the wrong side and pull the thread to gather. This is especially helpful when making the many circles required for the *Folkart Medallion* quilt.

8. Press the ¼" allowance over the cardboard template, applying a little spray starch to help set the crease. Continue around the entire edge of the motif, pressing in toward the center and applying spray starch as needed. Allow the fabric to cool before moving it from the pressing surface.

9. Carefully remove the cardboard template. The fabric should be fairly stiff and the allowance pressed firmly to the wrong side. The fabric shape is now ready to be applied to the background fabric, either by hand using a back whipstitch or by machine, using invisible machine appliqué techniques. Both methods are described below.

Hand Appliqué

The preferred stitch used for hand appliqué is a back whipstitch. Using a single strand of thread in a color to match the motif, secure one end with a knot. Bring the needle and thread up from the underside and out through the folded edge in the motif. Insert the tip of the needle a little below and slightly under the folded edge where the thread emerges. Without pulling the thread through, slant the needle and bring it to the top side

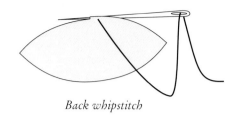

Back whipstitch

through the folded edge in the motif, approximately ¹⁄₁₆" away from the previous stitch. Pull the thread through. Continue stitching.

Invisible Machine Appliqué

Invisible machine appliqué is one method of machine stitching a motif to a background fabric. We feel it works well for many of the appliqué motifs in this book. In order to use this technique, it is necessary that you have a machine that will sew a blind hem stitch, as shown. It is always advisable to sew on a test piece first. Make any necessary adjustments in stitch length or width and determine the proper position of the foot along the folded edge of the motif.

1. Thread the top of your machine with 100% nylon invisible thread and the bobbin with machine embroidery thread. ✂ *HELPFUL HINT*: Check to see if your machine has additional thread guides on either the top or on the bobbin to achieve more tension, which may be required for this stitch.

2. Set your machine for a blind hem stitch. Place a motif under the

Invisible machine appliqué
Blind hem stitch

presser foot. Then use the hand wheel to determine the extreme right needle position. Turn the hand wheel to insert the needle into the background fabric just to the right of the folded edge of the motif. Lower the presser foot. Carefully stitch around the motif.

3. Continue turning the hand wheel. The straight stitches should be made tight against the folded edge. When the needle swings to the left, it should take a small bite over the folded edge and into the motif, as shown.

4. If this is occurring properly, continue stitching around the motif in a clockwise direction.

PRACTICE EXERCISE: APPLIQUÉ

Treasured Heart

▶ SUPPLIES:
- *5″ square of cotton fabric for heart*
- *6½″ square of cotton fabric for background*
- *Glass-head pins*
- *Light-colored thread for basting*
- *Small scissors*
- *Steam iron*
- *Pressing surface*
- *Light-colored towel*

- *Thread to match heart (for hand appliqué)*

–OR–

- *Sewing machine with 100% nylon invisible thread*

ALSO NEEDED:
Method One:
- *Plain paper*
- *Lead pencil*
- *Needle, No. 10 Betweens*

Method Two:
- *Plastic-coated freezer paper*
- *Ultra-fine permanent pen*

Method Three:
- *Template plastic*
- *Manila file folder*
- *Spray starch*

1. Use template pattern 11n at the back of the book for the heart motif.

2. Prepare the heart using one of the three methods described above. Refer to the hints in the method you are using for specific instructions on working with points and V's.

3. Apply the heart to the background fabric by either hand or machine. ✄ *HELPFUL HINT*: If you are applying the heart by hand, at the crook of the V bring the needle and thread to the front side. Use the tip of the needle to turn the allowance under along the other side of the V. Hold it in place with the thumb of your free hand. Make a small buttonhole stitch at the crook of the V by taking a stitch and then bringing the needle through the loop before pulling the thread all the way through. The buttonhole stitch helps to reinforce this area and prevent the allowance from coming out. Continue stitching until the motif is completely sewn to the background fabric.

4. For Method One: Remove the basting stitches, cut away the background fabric to within ¼″ of the stitching lines, and remove the paper pattern.

For Method Two: Carefully remove the freezer paper.

5. Give the block a final press.

Chapter 5

▼▼▼

SETTINGS AND BORDERS

Although settings and borders are two separate steps, we have combined them because both are thought about during this stage of quilt-making. With our students we spend one entire class arranging blocks on a design wall and experimenting with border possibilities. This is an exciting time in the quiltmaking process. Spend some time moving blocks around and working with border fabrics until you are comfortable with the final results. ✄ *HELPFUL HINT*: A reducing glass is useful during this process. An instant-print camera will also give you immediate feedback and help you make decisions.

Now that all your blocks are complete, you are ready to sew them together into a pleasing arrangement (called set or setting). Certainly you can use the same setting as shown in the photo of the pattern you have made, but why not try something a little different? Take a few minutes to read through the following descriptions and look at the examples. You might be inspired to stretch your creativity. Some of the simple ideas presented can make your quilt stand apart from all the rest.

Two types of settings are discussed and are used on many of the quilts in this book—straight and diagonal. Look at the *Jewel Box* quilts on the next page. The same blocks were used in

two different sets to illustrate the difference between straight and diagonal settings. ✄ *HELPFUL HINT*: Allow yourself some flexibility in fabric choices. Look at the *Jewel Box* diagonal setting. The side and corner triangles are from a different fabric than the one used in the pieced blocks—not because that was planned, but because the original fabric was no longer available. Often a subtle difference in backgrounds can add more interest. Do not panic. Try something else. You may like it!

A straight setting means that blocks are sewn together in straight horizontal and vertical rows. Look at the *Pieced Buttercup* quilt on page 46. Do not be confused because the colors form a diagonal pattern. It is still a straight setting. This arrangement works well for this pattern, producing a neat, clean look in the finished quilt.

A plain block (also called alternate block) can be added to the straight setting, as was done in the *Brass Rings* quilt on page 24. The simple addition of a black square gives definition to the pieced blocks. The pieced blocks form rings linking the blocks together. Adding alternate blocks is an easy way to enlarge a quilt while using fewer pieced blocks.

Another variation on the straight setting is used in the *Album Patch* quilt shown on page 52. Blocks are separated but unified by strips of red fabric

(called sashing or lattice). Sashing strips can be made from one of the fabrics used in your pieced blocks, or they can be of something entirely different that acts to unify the pieced blocks. When several hands go into the making of one quilt, such as the *Album Patch* friendship quilt, all finished blocks are often not the same size. That is no surprise, since we all have different cutting tools and sewing machines. Sashing strips will help set the blocks together and hide their differences. ✄ *HELPFUL HINT*: Rather than eliminate a block that is considerably smaller, simply add a narrow strip of background fabric around it before setting the blocks together. Then trim to the desired size. This adjustment strip will never be noticed in the finished quilt.

Sashing strips do not have to run both vertically and horizontally across the quilt. The *Apple Basket* quilt on page 76 uses only horizontal sashing strips. The floral fabric repeats some of the colors from the apples, adds more interest to the quilt, and increases the overall length.

Finally, alternate blocks and sashing can be combined to give another exciting design option. Look at Emily's *Stripped Nine-Patch* quilt on page 16. Emily is nine years old and this is her second quilt. The simple nine-patch block is joined by vertical pieced sashing strips. The block and the sashing are both easy enough for the beginner. The addition of alternate blocks means that fewer pieced blocks are required. This is an important consideration for a beginner. The use of the alternate block gives unity to Emily's quilt and the pieced sashing strips bring it up to her desired bed size.

A diagonal setting means that blocks are turned "on point" and sewn together in diagonal rows. This setting will not work well, however, for many representational blocks such as *Apple Basket* or *Courthouse Square*. These are better sewn in straight sets.

A simple and appropriate diagonal setting is used for the *Basket* quilt on page 35. This particular quilt also has sashing strips to separate and join the blocks together. Notice the small squares of black fabric at the intersections of the sashing strips: these are called posts and give yet another design option to the quilt. Posts are often helpful in keeping all of the

pieced blocks and sashing strips aligned.

The beautiful *Wild Goose Chase* on page 61 uses an alternate block with diagonal setting. In this instance the print fabric of the alternate blocks unifies the colors in the pieced blocks. Again, this is an easy way of using fewer pieced blocks to enlarge a quilt.

The Streak of Lightning setting used on the *Pine Trees* quilt on page 73 combines techniques from both diagonal and straight settings. The individual blocks are turned on point and sewn in units diagonally to form straight vertical rows. The vertical rows are joined to complete the quilt top. This setting is impressive and is much easier than it looks. Try using this variation on any blocks that work well turned on point.

Are you inspired and ready to begin arranging your own blocks? First, if all of your blocks are identical, as in the *Apple Basket* quilt, you can simply sew them together in horizon-

tal rows. Other quilts that have more assortment of blocks, especially the samplers, require planning for color placement and design balance before you join blocks together. We like to use a design wall (one that has been covered with felted fleece or flannel) for this purpose. The blocks will stick and can be easily moved around. A reducing glass will help you see color contrasts (light and dark) and spot those areas that may not be well balanced in color. Put the blocks onto the wall and move them around, experimenting with different arrangements. When you have decided on one you like, you will find specific instructions below for sewing the blocks together into the setting of your choice.

There is one last task you must perform before arranging your blocks. First, trim any loose threads from the pieced blocks and straighten the edges. Look on the back side to see that seams were not turned in the

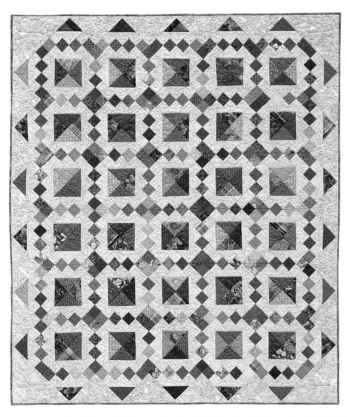

Jewel Box with diagonal setting (left) and straight setting (right), Diana McClun, Laura Nownes and friends; quilted by Kathy Sandbach

▼

wrong direction during sewing or pressing. If so, take a minute to correct them. Quilting will be easier if seams are facing the correct direction. Then measure to see that all blocks are the same size. Generally, if all of your blocks are the same pattern and you were consistent with your cutting and sewing, there will not be a problem. Even if all blocks measure 12¼" rather than the ideal of 12½", you can go on. Inconsistent sizes sometimes occur when you make sampler quilts, since many different patterns are used. If one block is considerably smaller, simply add 1"-wide strips of fabric around the edges. Then trim to the desired size.

When you have decided upon the setting for your blocks, use the following instructions. Then, if you are considering adding borders, continue to the discussion of borders below. If no border is to be added, run a stitching line just shy of ¼" around the edges of the quilt top. ☞ *WARNING*: Your quilt top is fragile at this stage. Do not handle it excessively or leave it on a design wall, as the fabric may distort.

2. Place the top block from Rows 1 and 2 right sides facing each other. Stitch them together along the right-hand edge.

3. Continue the chain of thread and sew the second blocks in Rows 1 and 2 together along the right-hand edge.

4. Continue chaining the remaining pair of blocks from Rows 1 and 2 together in the same manner. *Do not cut the chain of threads holding the pairs.*

5. With the first block on top, stack the blocks in Row 3. Then, with their right sides facing each other, stitch them to the blocks in Row 2, using the same method of chaining between rows.

6. Repeat this procedure for the remaining rows.

7. Press the new seams in each horizontal row in opposite directions, as shown, to prevent bulk when you join the rows.

8. Sew the horizontal rows together, placing pins at the intersections of their seams.

9. Press the new seams to one direction.

10. Give the quilt top a final press.

Step 1

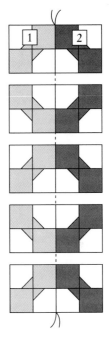

Step 4

▶ STRAIGHT SETTING

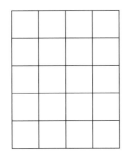

Sewing Blocks Together

1. With the first block in each row on top, stack the blocks from Row 1 and Row 2, as shown. ✄ *HELPFUL HINT*: Mark the number of each row onto a piece of paper to eliminate any mix-up, in case you are interrupted during this process.

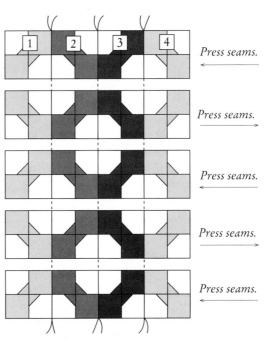

Press seams.

Press seams.

Press seams.

Press seams.

Press seams.

Step 7

▼

Adding Sashing Strips to a Straight Setting

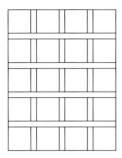

1. While all the blocks are arranged on the floor or your design wall, determine the total number of vertical (short) and horizontal (long) sashing strips needed for your quilt. Refer to the diagram for help.

2. Vertical sashing strips are cut the desired finished width plus ½″. The length is the same measurement as your blocks.

3. Join the blocks in the top row to the sashing strips, as shown. Press the seams toward the sashing strips.

4. Sew vertical sashing strips to the blocks in the remaining rows. Press. Then take the measurement across one of the horizontal rows. This measurement will be the length of the horizontal sashing strips.

5. Pin and then sew a sashing strip between each pair of rows. Ease if necessary to be sure that all ends are even with each other.

✄ *HELPFUL HINT*: When joining rows, check to be sure that vertical sashing strips are aligned. Pin to secure before sewing.

6. Press the seams toward the sashing strips. Then give the quilt top a final press.

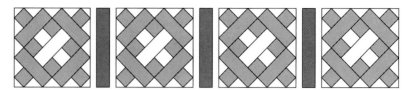

Step 3

Steps 3–4

Adding Sashing and Posts to a Straight Setting

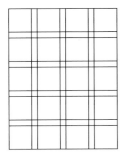

Squares of fabric, called posts, can be used to join sashing pieces. The measurement of the posts is the same as the width of the sashing strips. All sashing strips (both vertical and horizontal) are cut the same size.

1. Follow Steps 1-3 of "Adding Sashing Strips to a Straight Setting."

2. Join the required number of sashing strips to posts to make horizontal sashing strips, as shown. Press seams toward sashing strips.

3. Sew vertical sashing strips to the blocks in the remaining rows. Press. Then take the measurement across one of the horizontal rows. This measurement will be the length of the horizontal sashing strips.

4. Pin and then sew a sashing strip between each pair of rows. Ease if necessary to be sure that all ends are even with each other.

✀ *HELPFUL HINT*: When joining rows, check to be sure that vertical sashing strips are aligned. Pin to secure before sewing.

5. Press the seams toward the sashing strips. Then give the quilt top a final press.

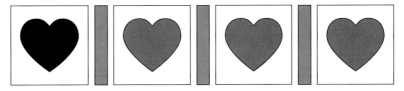

Step 1

Step 2

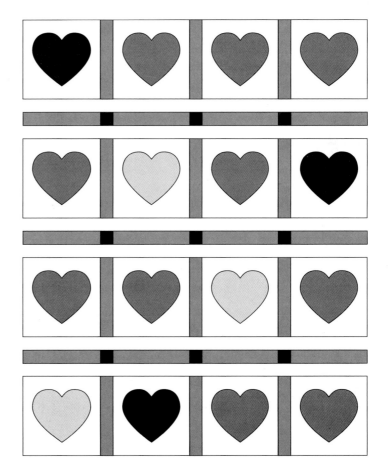

Step 3

▶ DIAGONAL SETTING

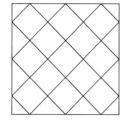

Sewing Blocks Together

Side and corner triangles are required when you sew blocks in a diagonal set. The cut sizes of all of the side and corner triangles for the patterns in this book are deliberately a little too large. This will allow you to trim and straighten the edges of the quilt top before adding borders or binding.

1. Lay out all of the quilt blocks, side and corner triangles on the floor or on your design wall in the desired arrangement. If using alternate blocks, place them in the appropriate positions. Be sure to place side triangles exactly as shown in the diagram. Pin pieces of paper marked #1, #2, #3, etc., on the side triangle of each diagonal row.

2. Sew the side triangles to opposite sides of the pieced block in Row 1. Refer to the diagram for help. Then press these seams to one direction.

3. Stitch the side triangles and the blocks in Row 2 together. Then press these seams opposite to the seams pressed in Row 1.

4. Stitch the blocks and side triangles in the remaining rows together in the same manner.

5. Join Row 1 to Row 2, placing pins at the seam intersections to hold them secure.

6. Add Row 3, Row 4, etc. Then sew on the four corner triangles.

7. Take the quilt top to the cutting board and use the wide plastic ruler and rotary cutter to straighten the edges of the quilt top and remove the excess fabric to within ⅜" of the cor-

ners of the pieced blocks. When adding a border or binding, allow ⅜" rather than the usual ¼". This will keep you from cutting off the corner points of the blocks. Check to see that opposite sides are the same measurement and that corners make accurate 90° angles. Be careful not to stretch the edges.

8. Give the quilt top a final press.

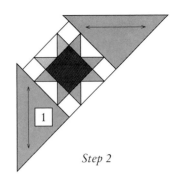

Step 2

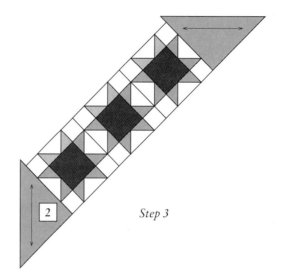

Step 3

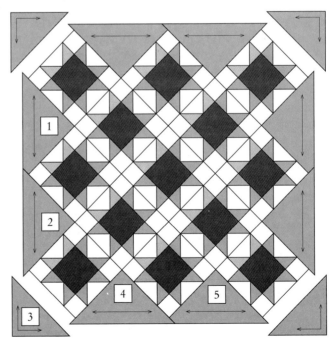

Steps 5–6

Adding Sashing Strips to a Diagonal Setting

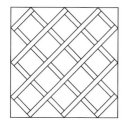

NOTE: Side and corner triangles must be cut larger if sashing strips are added.

1. While all the blocks are arranged on the floor or your design wall, determine the total number of A and B sashing strips needed for your quilt. Refer to the diagram above for help.

2. The A sashing strips are cut the desired finished width plus ½". The length is the same measurement as your blocks.

3. Sew A sashing strips to both sides of the block in Row 1. Press the seams toward the sashing strips. Then take the measurement across this block plus sashing strips. Cut a B sashing strip this measurement and sew it to the top of the block.

4. Sew the side triangles to the sashing strips to complete Row 1, as shown.

5. Sew A sashing strips, B sashing strips, then side triangles, using the same method as described above, for the remaining rows. Note that the center row will have a sashing strip on both top and bottom.

6. Join the diagonal rows, placing pins to keep the A sashing strips aligned.

7. Sew the corner triangles to complete the quilt top.

8. Take the quilt top to the cutting board and use the wide plastic ruler and rotary cutter to straighten the edges of the quilt top and remove the excess fabric to within ⅜" of the corners of the sashing strips. When adding a border or a binding, allow ⅜" rather than the usual ¼". This will keep you from cutting off the corner points of the blocks. Check to see that opposite sides are the same measurement and that corners are at right angles. Be careful not to stretch the edges.

9. Give the quilt top a final press.

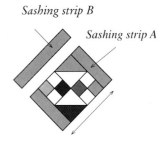

Sashing strip B

Sashing strip A

Step 3

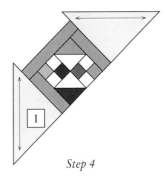

Step 4

Step 5

Adding Sashing and Posts to a Diagonal Setting

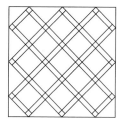

Squares of fabric (called posts) can be used to join sashing strips, as shown.

1. While all the blocks are arranged on the floor or your design wall, determine the total number of sashing strips and posts needed for your quilt. Refer to the diagram for help. Note that all sashing strips are the same measurement.

2. Cut the sashing strips the desired finished width plus ½". Cut the posts; the measurement of the posts is the same as the width of your sashing strips.

3. Sew sashing strips to both sides of the block in Row 1.

4. Sew posts to opposite ends of one sashing strip. Then sew this unit to the top edge of Row 1, as shown.

5. Sew the side triangles to complete Row 1, as shown.

6. Sew sashing strips at the ends and between the blocks in Row 2.

7. Join three sashing strips to four posts, alternating posts and sashing strips. Then lay this unit right sides facing each other along the top edge of Row 2. Align the posts with the sashing strips and secure with pins. Sew.

8. Continue in this manner with the remaining rows.

9. Join the diagonal rows, carefully aligning the posts with the sashing strips.

10. Follow Steps 7-10 of "Adding Sashing to a Diagonal Setting."

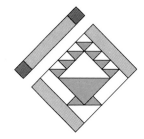

Step 4

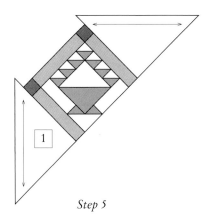

Step 5

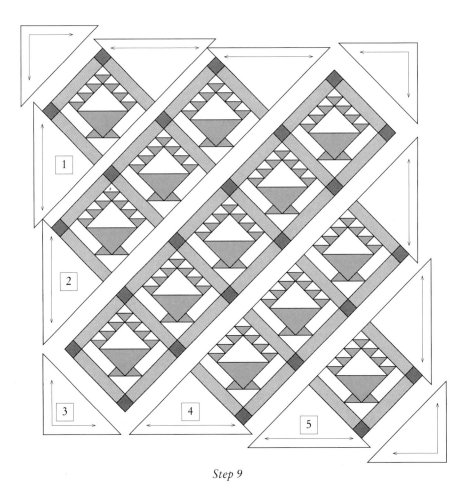

Step 9

136
▼

Streak of Lightning Setting

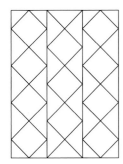

The dramatic Streak of Lightning setting that was used on the *Pine Trees* quilt on page 73 combines techniques from both the straight and diagonal sets. Blocks are joined to triangles to make diagonal units, which are then sewn into vertical rows. It is often difficult to see the seams joining the rows, since the setting creates such a strong zigzag effect.

This setting appears more difficult than it actually is and can be striking for any blocks that work well turned on point. Notice that half-blocks are required at the top and bottom on alternate vertical rows. Unfortunately, you cannot simply make one block and cut it in half diagonally, as there would not be seam allowances. You must make half-blocks that include seam allowance along the diagonal (see page 75).

Take time while sewing, pressing, and straightening the edges to avoid stretching. Also, to prevent stretching along the edges of the vertical rows, it is important to use the straight grain of the fabric along the edges. For the large triangles, cut squares of fabric into quarters diagonally, as shown.

The cut size of the squares is the diagonal measurement of the blocks plus 1½″. For the small triangles required at the top and bottom of alternate rows, cut squares of fabric in half diagonally, as shown.

The cut size of the squares is one-half the diagonal measurement of the blocks plus 1½″. Both the large and small triangles are cut slightly larger

than needed to allow for trimming and straightening the edges before joining rows or adding borders.

1. Arrange the blocks on the floor or on a design wall, placing large and small triangles where appropriate.

Refer to the diagram for help.

2. Working vertically, sew triangles to the pieced blocks in units, as shown.

3. Join the units to make vertical rows, as shown.

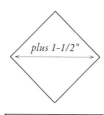

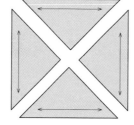

Cutting large triangles

Cutting small triangles

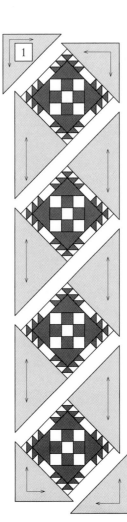

Steps 2–3

▼

4. Trim and straighten the edges of the rows: lay a row on top of your cutting board with the right side facing up. Use your wide plastic ruler and rotary cutter to trim the edges of the row, ⅜" beyond the corners of the pieced blocks. (You must allow ⅜" rather than the usual ¼" to prevent corners from being cut off when rows are joined.) Take your time to measure and cut accurately. To do so, place the line marked on your ruler for ⅜" evenly with the corners of two blocks, as shown.

Trim the excess fabric. Slide the ruler to the left, placing the ⅜" marking beyond the corner of the next block. Trim the excess fabric.

Continue to slide the ruler and cut along the entire length of the row.

5. Trim the opposite side using the same procedure.

6. Trim the ends, using the 90° marking on the ruler to be certain that corners are square.

7. Trim the remaining rows in the same manner.

8. Mark the center point of each large triangle with pins along the edge, as shown. Then join vertical rows together, matching pins with the corners of the adjoining pieced blocks.

9. Give the quilt top a final press.

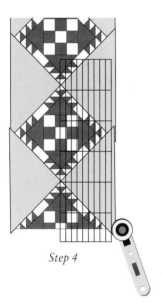

Step 4

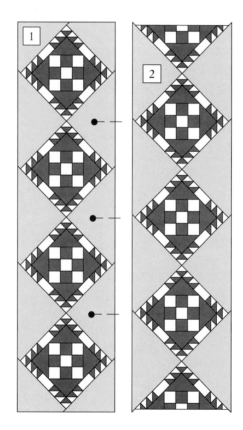

Step 8

▶ BORDERS

How many times have you finished sewing your blocks together and asked yourself, "Does my quilt need a border?" Sometimes this is a difficult question and the answer can be simply a matter of preference. We have given many ideas and examples from our quilts to help you through this decision-making process.

We generally wait until after deciding on a setting before choosing a border fabric. The quilt often takes on a different look—perhaps more blue than you had envisioned. Rather than be disappointed with your border fabric, please wait. When the blocks are arranged, you can pin different lengths of fabric around the edges to see which one best complements your quilt. Also, you may want your border narrower or wider than those suggested in the yardage charts in order to fit a particular wall space or bed size. This gives you the option of making any desired adjustments.

Often making a border is as involved and time-consuming as making the pieced blocks. It might be easier to stop and not add any borders. We realized this after sewing the *Martha Washington Star* blocks together. However, the pieced border added many more hours and, in the end, it was definitely worth the time. Lay pieces of paper over the borders of this quilt as shown on page 83 and you can see that it was a likely candidate for borders. The quilt without a border seems incomplete. At such a point you will know it is time to experiment with different border possibilities.

Some patterns look complete without the addition of borders, such as *Lady of the Lake* on page 68. However, borders can enhance a quilt pattern, increase the size, and bring it up to a desired wall space or bed size. The possibilities are endless. Try some of the ones used on our quilts, or design one of your own.

Types of Borders

Single strips of fabric add a frame to your quilt top, such as the simple border on the *Jewel Box* quilt on page 130. A single strip can be used to separate the pieced blocks from a pieced border, such as the narrow pink strip on the *Four-Patch* quilt on page 12. A border-printed fabric was used on the *Treasured Hearts* quilt on page 30. There are many attractive border-printed fabrics available for this purpose.

Pieced borders do not always have to be involved and time-consuming to be effective. Consider the simple checkerboard border on the *Courthouse Square* quilt on page 79 or the pieced squares on the *Four-Patch* quilt on page 12. You can see what a little extra time spent on border treatment adds to the overall finished look.

Try repeating one of the elements contained in your pieced blocks. You may already have several leftover units and need only make a few more for the borders. The *Apple Basket* quilt on page 76 is an example. Additional half-square triangle units were made and added to those left over from the baskets. The units were then sewn into groups of four to make a simple yet effective pieced border for this quilt. One of the easiest pieced borders is called the sawtooth border, made up entirely of half-square triangle units. Look at how effective the double sawtooth border is on the *Pieced Buttercup* quilt on page 46 and also on the *Sailboat* quilt on page 58.

Measuring Borders

If you have decided that your quilt needs a border, regardless of type, it is important to determine the length of the border strips. We cannot stress enough the importance of measuring your quilt top *before* attaching borders to determine the exact length needed for border strips.

☞ *WARNING*: Do not simply cut border strips and sew them to the quilt without first measuring. If you do, you could have rippled edges or splayed corners.

Lay the quilt top out on a flat surface and use a plastic or metal tape measure to determine dimension A (the longer dimension) and B (the shorter dimension) across the center. Write these figures down. Measure the center of your quilt from edge to edge. This is more accurate than measuring the sides, where stretching occurs.

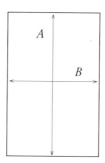

Cutting Border Strips

If you are cutting border strips crosswise, cut the necessary pieces, referring to the border section of the cutting chart for strip width. Remove the selvages, then join strips together to equal the lengths of the sides of your quilt top.

If you are using lengthwise strips, remove one selvage edge from the fabric, then cut four lengthwise strips. Refer to the border section of the cutting chart for strip width.

If you are using a directional fabric or a border-printed fabric, be careful to cut straight along the printed design.

Attaching Straight Borders

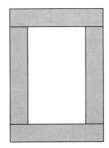

1. Cut two strips of fabric for the borders the desired width (plus ½″) by the measurement determined above for dimension A.

2. Place pins at the center points of the border strips and also at the center points along sides A of the quilt top.

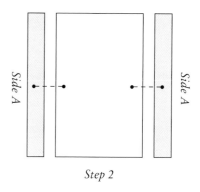

Step 2

3. With right sides facing, lay these border strips on each A side of the quilt top, matching pins at center points and opposite ends. Use more pins to hold the borders in place. Sew with the border strips on top, as they are more stable than the pieced quilt top and less likely to stretch. Ease in any fullness if necessary. ✂ *HELPFUL HINT*: Seam allowances on the edges of the quilt top on the underside may tend to turn in the wrong direction while you are sewing. Use the tip of a seam ripper to hold them in place.

4. Press the border strip flat on the wrong side. Then fold it over the stitching line and press.

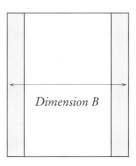

Step 5

5. Lay the quilt top out on a flat surface and use a plastic or metal tape measure to determine the new dimension B (which includes the A border strips) across the center.

6. Cut two strips of fabric for the side B borders the desired width (plus ½″) by the measurement determined in Step 5.

7. Place pins at the center points of these border strips and also at the center points along sides B of the quilt top.

8. Attach these border strips to the quilt top, using the same method described in Steps 3 and 4 above.

9. Give the quilt top a final press.

You can now attach additional borders, using the same technique. *Finish one border before you add another.*

Attaching Mitered Borders

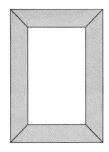

1. Using the figure determined above in "Measuring Borders," cut two strips of fabric for the side A borders the desired width plus ½″. The length of these strips will be dimension A plus two times the cut width. Then add an additional 4″ for working allowance. Let's simplify this with an example: If dimension A is 60″ and the strip width is 4″, then 60″ + 2 times 4″ is 68″; add the working allowance of 4″, for a total cut length of 72″.

2. Repeat the same procedure of measuring and cutting strips for sides B, using dimension B.

3. Place pins at the center points of the two A border strips. Measure out from the pins in each direction a distance equal to one-half the A

dimension. Place pins at these points to mark the corners. Also place pins at the center points along sides A of the quilt top, as shown.

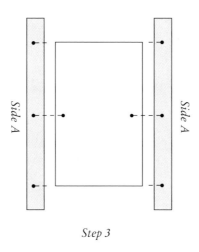

Step 3

4. With right sides facing, lay the A border strips on each A side of the quilt top. Match pins with corners and at the center points. Use more pins to hold the borders in place. Beginning and ending ¼″ *from each corner,* stitch the A borders to the quilt top, with the border strip on top, as it is more stable than the pieced quilt top and less likely to stretch. Ease in any fullness if necessary. ✂ *HELPFUL HINT:* The tip of a seam ripper will help keep any seam allowances on the edges of the quilt top on the underside from being turned in the wrong direction while you are sewing. There will be a generous amount of fabric beyond the quilt top at both ends of the borders. You need this fabric to miter the corners. *Do not cut it off.*

5. Mark the center points on the other two borders. From both directions, measure one-half the B dimension. Mark those points with pins.

6. Pin the center points along sides B of the quilt top.

7. Sew these borders to the quilt top, as in Step 4.

8. Working on one corner of the quilt at your pressing surface, bring the unsewn border ends out straight,

overlapping the end of A over the end of B, as shown.

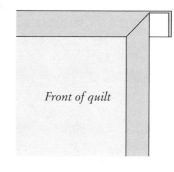

Step 9

9. Lift the A strip and fold it at a 45° angle under *only itself,* as shown. Check that the corner is square. Use the corner of your wide plastic ruler, and lay the 45° angle over the diagonal fold. When the angles are accurate, press to set.

10. On the wrong side, place pins near the pressed fold in the corner to secure the border strips.

11. Wrong side up, stitch along the folded line in the corner. Carefully stitch only to the previous stitching line, to avoid gaps or puckers.

12. Trim excess fabric from the borders, as shown.

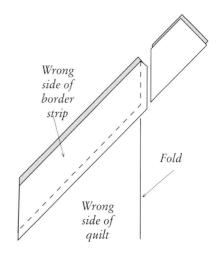

Step 12

13. Press on the right side.

14. Complete the other corners in the same way.

HELPFUL HINT: Mitered corners are an important focal point of border-printed fabric. To make them symmetrical, place a similar design at the center point of each side. If you allow extra length on the border strips, you can try different corner options.

Attaching Pieced Borders

Many quiltmakers avoid using pieced borders because they are unsure how to calculate the size of the pieced unit and the number of units required for each side. They also worry about the corners. You can start by dividing the measurement (length or width) of your quilt by the size of the unit you wish to make, to determine the number of units needed for that side. Let us warn you, however, that even with the most accurate of calculations, it is rare that what is true on paper remains true with fabric. There are variations in cutting and sewing, and the slightest difference will cause a pieced border to be a little too long or short. This was the case when Laura attached the final sawtooth border to the *Folkart Medallion* quilt. All calculations showed that 36 half-square triangle units were required for each side. When 36 units were sewn together, however, the pieced strip was one unit too long for a side. Although it may be off just one thread width in either your cutting or sewing, when multiplied by the number of seams required in the pieced border strip (in this case 35 seams) the difference adds up.

When sewing the border strip to the quilt top, pin first to ease in fullness. This became crucial with the *Apple Basket* quilt on page 76. Another option is to take a *slightly* deeper seam in one or more of the seams along the pieced strip before attaching it to the quilt.

Leftover units from the pieced blocks often make interesting bor-

Pieced border (Bow Tie)

ders. This is what we did on the *Apple Basket* and *Bow Tie* quilts. Although the border units fit nicely onto each side, you will notice that opposite corners differ on the *Bow Tie*. This possibly could have been avoided if we had enlarged the quilt by adding a strip of fabric (called an adjustment strip) before attaching the pieced border. We liked the look as it was and decided to leave it. However, we did add an adjustment strip on both the *Apple Basket* and the *Six-Pointed Star Variation* before attaching the pieced border. Here are the steps we took to make the pieced border fit.

1. Make a quick calculation to determine approximately how many units are needed for each side of the quilt. Let's use the example of a 60″ x 80″ quilt with a 2″ finished half-square triangle unit for a sawtooth border. If you divide 60″ by 2″ you find you need 30 units for each short side, and dividing 80″ by 2″ gives 40 units for each long side.

2. Lay the half-square triangle units around the outer edge of the quilt top to determine the direction you

want them pointing on each side. Then sew them together in strips: two strips of 30 each and two strips of 40 each. Press the pieced strips.

3. Lay the strips alongside the edges of the quilt top. Are they exactly the right length, or a little too short or too long? If they fit perfectly, then you can simply pin and sew the pieced strips to the quilt top, using the methods described in Steps 2-5 and 8-10 of "Attaching Straight Borders." Be sure to add one unit to the end of each side B pieced strip for the corners, as shown in the diagram.

Will removing one unit or adding one unit solve the problem? If neither will work, then consider a narrow adjustment strip between the quilt top and the pieced border.

4. Cut strips of fabric wider than appear to be needed to fit the pieced border to the quilt top. You will remove the excess when the pieced strips are pinned and then sewn in place to fit exactly.

You are now ready to begin the quilting process.

141

▼

Chapter 6

QUILTING

Quilting stitches have been used for centuries in clothing, armor, and bedding. The stitches are practical, in that they hold the layers together for warmth and durability. They also contribute great textural interest, and they help the colored fabrics to absorb or reflect more light, adding highlights and shadows. Additionally, they provide the quiltmaker with another avenue to explore and express decorative creativity. Most quilts contain three layers (top, batting, backing) held together by stitches—running stitch for hand quilting and straight stitch for machine quilting.

We have invited four experts to share their expertise with you: Adele Ingraham and Anna Venti for hand work, JoAnn Manning and Kathy Sandbach for machine work. JoAnn and Kathy spent days studying the quilt tops we sent before they hit upon the right designs to co-ordinate with the pieced surfaces and enrich them. Their imagination and experience produced the works of quilting art you see in this book. Executing fine quilting designs takes practice, but you soon find yourself attuned to the rhythms, and your skill flourishes.

Hand quilting is more popular now than it has been for some years, as quilters seek a calm diversion from the hectic pressures of our society and find it in the rhythms of hand and needle. In Anna Venti's work, the hand stitches follow an orderly layout that marries the motifs and filling stitches to the overall style of the quilt top. Marian Ritchie, in *Interlocked Squares,* chose large areas of solid colors for the elaborate wreaths and feathers that showcase her fine, even hand work—more suitable for "best quilts" than for everyday, utilitarian ones.

In the past, most quilts were quilted by hand, whether pieced by hand or machine. Today's quiltmaker has the advantage of choosing either method of quilting, or a combination of both. Sally Barlow began quilting her sampler by hand but, as a deadline caught up with her, she finished the border quilting by machine.

Learn to experiment with the many ways you can use the quilting lines, and remain flexible. Aim always toward developing your textural composition, and thereby enriching your quilt. If you love the designs we present, feel free to copy them; we also encourage you wholeheartedly to experiment.

✂ *HELPFUL HINT*: If your quilt top has been folded for some time, give it a good press to remove the creases or wrinkles.

▶ QUILTING DESIGNS

Intricate patterns, such as the wreath in the larger corner squares of the *Star of Bethlehem* quilt on page 86, should be marked onto the quilt top before you begin layering and basting. There are many plastic quilting templates available for this purpose: they are pre-cut, so you can easily transfer the lines to your quilt top, and there are a variety of sizes and designs. Look for a pattern that enhances your quilt top and fills the space.

A pre-cut quilting stencil requires less work than tracing a pattern from a book and then cutting your own plastic templates. Some quilting patterns were designed specifically for this book by two of our machine quilters, JoAnn Manning and Kathy Sandbach, with a machine quilter in mind. However, they are also appropriate for hand quilting.

It is often difficult for a beginning quilter to decide on the design to use for quilting. So we have included diagrams of many of the designs used in our sample quilts. Most of them are very simple but effective and can easily be marked onto your quilt top.

If you have selected a design that must be marked *before* layering and basting, these steps will help you:

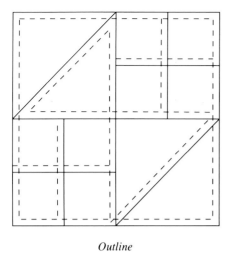

Outline

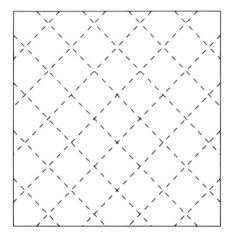

Cross-hatch or square diamonds

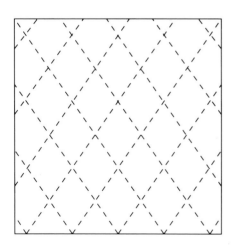

Hanging diamonds

1. Lay the quilt top with the right side facing you on a flat surface. Center the quilting template over the area to be marked. Secure the corners of the template with tape to prevent slipping.

2. Use a marking pencil (light-colored for dark fabrics) or chalk marker to lightly transfer a thin, sharp line to the quilt top. ✂ *HELPFUL HINT*: There are a variety of marking tools available for this purpose: dressmaker's pencils, soapstone markers, and water-soluble marking pens. If you choose one of the water-soluble pens, it is important that you follow label directions and keep the marked quilt out of the sun to prevent heat-setting the markings. Also, the quilt must be washed after quilting to remove all lines completely. It is always best to test the tool on your fabric before marking: you do not want the lines to rub off and disappear as you quilt, nor do you want them to be permanent. If you will be machine quilting, however, the lines must be darker than for hand quilting.

3. Mark all the required lines. Not all quilting lines need to be marked onto the quilt top before it is layered and basted to the batting and backing. Straight-line stitching, such as outline stitching for background quilting (cross-hatch or hanging diamonds, for example) can be marked as you quilt, using a small ruler and marking tool.

▶ BACKING FABRIC

Backing can be constructed from one or several fabrics pieced together. It can be something very individual and special. It is always fun to turn a quilt to its "wrong" side and be surprised by the backing. The backing fabric should be at least 2″ larger all the way around than the quilt top. To prepare your backing fabric:

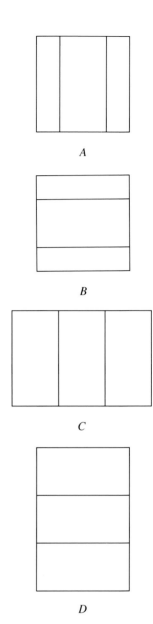

A

B

C

D

1. If your backing fabric is stiff, it is a good idea to wash it before layering and basting, to make quilting easier.

2. Cut the selvages off, as they are tightly woven and difficult to quilt through.

3. Cut the required number of lengths of backing fabric for the quilt you are making. Cutting charts will refer you to diagrams on this page that indicate the most efficient way to piece the backing lengths. When two lengths are required (diagrams A and B), the finished quilt will lay better if one length is cut in half lengthwise and then sewn to opposite sides, as shown.

4. Sew the pieces together as indicated. ✂ *HELPFUL HINT*: Diagrams A, B, C, and D are helpful when piecing your backing fabric.

5. Sew the pieces together. Then press the seams *open*: open seams are easier to quilt through.

▶ BATTING

There are many battings available. You need to choose a good quality that is neither too stiff nor too thick. We like a flat, traditional look for our finished quilts. To achieve this, we prefer a low-loft bonded 100% polyester batting for hand quilting. For best results, the quilting stitches should be no more than 2″ to 3″ apart. Our preference for machine quilting is a 100% cotton batting. Some brands require pre-washing, and you should follow the manufacturer's instructions. Quilting stitches on cotton batting should be no more than ½″ to 2″ apart.

▶ LAYERING AND BASTING

For hand quilting, using a hoop, a PVC frame, or a frame with round poles

▶ SUPPLIES:
- *Masking tape*
- *Batting*
- *Glass-head pins*
- *Darning needle*
- *Light-colored thread for basting*
- *Scissors*

Use a large utility table (not a dining table) or floor for this process, as the needle will scratch the surface.

1. With the wrong side facing you, lay the prepared backing on a flat surface. Use masking tape to secure the edges. Be sure the backing fabric is taut.

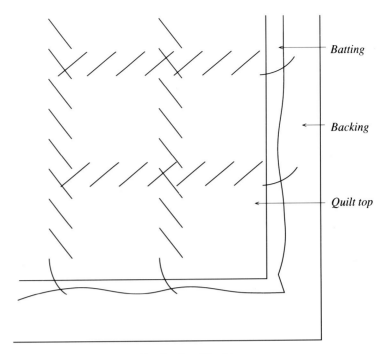

Basting in a 6″ grid

2. Lay the batting on top of the backing fabric. Smooth out any folds or creases.

3. With the right side facing you, center the quilt top over the batting. ✂ *HELPFUL HINT*: If you are using a directional printed fabric for the backing, check that your quilt top is facing the desired direction.

4. Starting in the center and working out toward the edges, use glass-head pins to secure all three layers,

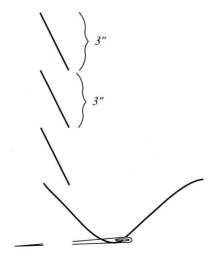

Diagonal basting stitch

placing pins approximately 8″ apart.

5. Thread a darning needle with approximately 4 feet of light-colored thread. Secure one end with a knot.

6. Starting from the center of the quilt and working toward the edges, stitch the layers together with a long diagonal basting stitch. The stitches should form a grid approximately 6″ apart, as shown.

Diagonal basting stitch: Long, parallel diagonal stitches on the right side of the quilt.

7. Remove the pins and masking tape. Trim the batting to within ½″ of the quilt top.

8. Trim the backing to within 2″ of the quilt top. Then fold the excess backing in half, so that the raw edge of the backing comes up even with the raw edge of the quilt top. Fold the backing again, bringing the fold of backing over the edge of the quilt top ¼″. Secure the folded edge of the backing to the quilt top with glass-head pins all the way around the quilt. Use a long running stitch to sew this folded edge through all layers, removing the pins as you sew.

This step keeps the edge of the quilt top from stretching and raveling and prevents the batting from linting while you are quilting. This is *not* the finished edge of the quilt. A separate binding will be attached when the quilting is done; it is explained in the next chapter.

Using a Square Board Frame

Square board frames are often used for basting quilts that will be hand quilted. They hold the layers very taut, but they do require a larger work space than a frame with rounded poles. You can easily make your own, following the steps given below.

▶ SUPPLIES:
- *Four one-by-two boards*
- *Four 2½″ C-clamps*
- *Muslin (the length of the sides of your backing fabric)*
- *Staple gun*
- *T-square*
- *Four chairs or stands*
- *Glass-head pins*
- *Light-colored thread for basting*
- *Hand-sewing needle*

1. Make a frame using the boards. Secure the corners with C-clamps, as shown. The inner size of the frame should be the same measurement as your backing fabric. Position the frame at a height convenient for you while seated. Chairs or stands work well for this.

2. Cut four pieces of muslin, each 5″ wide by the inner measurement of the boards.

3. Fold the muslin strips in half lengthwise and press.

4. Place the raw edges of the muslin down the center of each board and secure with the staple gun, as shown.

5. Mark the center points on each muslin strip and also points halfway between those centers and the ends of the muslin strips, as shown. Then divide the backing fabric in the same manner and mark the points with pins.

6. With the wrong side of the backing up, match the centers of the backing with the centers of the muslin strips. Secure with pins.

7. Pin the corners of the backing to the muslin strips. Then pin the remaining length of the backing to the muslin strips. The backing should be taut, and the distance from the corner to the center points the same on opposite sides.

8. Carefully place the batting over the backing, smoothing out any folds.

9. Mark the center point on each side of the quilt top with a pin. Then find the midway point between each pin and the corner of the quilt top. With the right side up, carefully lay the quilt top over the batting. The center points should be in line with the center points on the muslin strips.

10. Use a T-square to be certain that your quilt top is square. Then place pins perpendicular to the edge of the quilt top around the outer edges of the quilt top, through both the batting and backing layers.

11. Run a basting stitch around the edges of the quilt top. Then remove the pins.

You are ready to begin hand quilting. Start from the edges and work toward the center; release the C-clamps and roll the top boards toward you as needed.

For machine quilting

▶ SUPPLIES:
- *Spray starch*
- *Steam iron*
- *Ironing board*
- *Picnic tablecloth clamps*
- *Glass-head pins*
- *Steel safety pins (No. 1)*

1. Apply spray starch to the backing fabric to keep it smooth and taut and prevent it from stretching during quilting. Press.

2. With the wrong side facing up, pull the backing out straight and taut. You can use a large utility table and hold the edges with picnic tablecloth clamps, or use a square board quilt frame.

3. Carefully lay the batting over the backing, and smooth out any folds.

4. With the right side up, lay the quilt top over the batting. Smooth it. Be certain that edges are straight and corners are accurate 90° angles. Pull

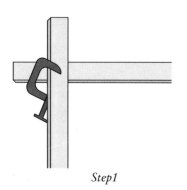

Step 1

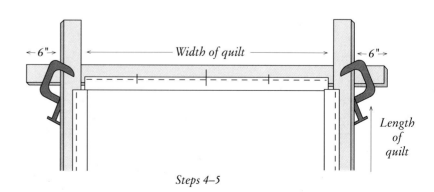

Steps 4–5

Using a Square Board Frame

the top as taut as the backing, then secure it with clamps (if using a table) or with pins (if using a frame).

5. Starting on one side and working across to the opposite side, use safety pins to secure all three layers, placing pins approximately 3″ to 4″ apart. The more intricate quilting designs require closer pinning. Avoid placing pins directly over seams or areas that will receive quilting lines.

6. Trim the batting to within 1″ of the edge of the quilt top.

You are ready to begin the quilting process.

▶ HAND QUILTING

In order to quilt to the edges, you must add a muslin extension around the quilt. You will find that 6″-wide strips work well.

If you are using a hoop, place the smaller inner ring on a flat surface. With the right side facing up, lay the area of your quilt to be quilted over the ring. Generally you will begin quilting in the center of the quilt and work out to the edges. Place the larger outer ring on top of the quilt. Use both hands to push the outer ring down even with the inner ring. Use the palm of your hand to push against the quilt to release some of the tension. Tighten the screw on the outer ring. The quilt should feel spongy.

Although we secure the ends of the quilting thread with knots, we prefer to have as few knots as possible. Take a minute to evaluate the area to be quilted before cutting your thread.

Lay the thread along the lines to be quilted (no more than 38″). Add 6″ to the length, then cut. You can eliminate two knots for each length of thread if you will follow the easy steps described in this example of the *Row House* quilt block.

▶ SUPPLIES:
- *Quilting thread*
- *Needle (No. 9 or 10 Betweens)*
- *Thimble*
- *Finger cot*
- *Small scissors*

1. Thread your small Betweens needle with quilting thread. Do not knot the end.

2. Place a thimble on the center finger of your quilting hand and a finger cot on the pointer finger of the same

Hand quilting (Baskets)

hand. ✂ *HELPFUL HINT*: Finger cots can be purchased at your local drug store. They are useful as grabbers for pulling the needle and thread through the three layers.

3. Insert the needle and thread at point X, going through all layers. Pull up only one-half of the length. The center of the thread is at point X. You are holding the threaded half, and the other half hangs loose.

4. Take a small backstitch through the quilt top and batting layer only. Stitch along the upper edge of the mountain and roof with small running stitches going through all layers. End at a seam intersection. Then thread the other half of thread and quilt along the side and bottom edges of the block, as shown.

The Quilting Stitch

1. Place the tip of the center finger of your free hand on the backside of the quilt, directly under the area to be quilted.

2. Insert the tip of the needle straight down into the quilt and push through with your thimble. As soon as the tip touches your finger, immediately bring the tip of the needle up to the front side. To do this, position the thumb of your quilting hand approximately 1″ ahead of the point

where the needle is inserted. Then, pressing your thumb against the quilt and pushing the needle at an upward angle with your thimble finger, bring the tip of the needle up. As soon as the tip of the needle is visible, insert it again through all layers, just a little ahead of where it came up. Continue with this up-and-down rocking motion until there are about four stitches on the tip of the needle. To keep the stitches small, it is important to work only on the tip of the needle. Then bring the needle and thread all the way through. Continue stitching across the line in the same manner.

3. Ideally, you want to end the stitching line at an intersection, but this is not always possible. To end the thread, take a small backstitch through the top layer only. Pull the needle and thread to the top side. Wrap the thread around the needle two times and, holding the wraps with your free hand, pull the needle through. This will create a French knot close to the surface of the quilt. At the point where the thread emerged, insert the needle into the batting layer and gently tug to pop the knot below the surface of the quilt top. Bring the needle and thread out approximately ½″ away, and cut the thread.

4. When you have finished all the quilting lines, run a machine stitching line ¼″ away from the edge all the way around the quilt.

5. You are ready to go on to the next chapter and bind your quilt.

✂ *HELPFUL HINTS*: 1. Keep the tension of the stitches even, neither too tight nor too loose.

2. Move the position of the needle on the thread often to prevent shredding.

3. If seam intersections are too bulky to stitch through, simply slip the needle under the seam into the batting layer and pull it out. Then fill in the empty space on top with running stitches so it will appear as a continuous line of quilting. Or, you can make one stitch at a time (called stab stitching).

4. Apply even amounts of quilting in each block to avoid buckling and allow the quilt to lay flat.

5. Stitch along the seams joining the blocks.

6. Clip the basting threads as you come to them.

7. To prevent creases in your quilt, always remove it from the hoop when you are finished quilting.

▶ MACHINE QUILTING

▶ **SUPPLIES:**
- *Sewing machine*
- *Cotton thread*
- *100% nylon invisible thread designed for machine quilting (optional)*
- *Walking foot or open darning foot*
- *Small scissors*

It is important that your machine be in good running order so you will not become frustrated with machine quilting. Since sewing machines vary, it is best to make a sample piece and experiment with stitch length and tension before beginning on your

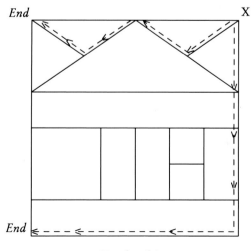

Hand quilting

▼

Above: Machine quilting (Jewel Box)*, Below: Machine quilting* (Four-Patch)

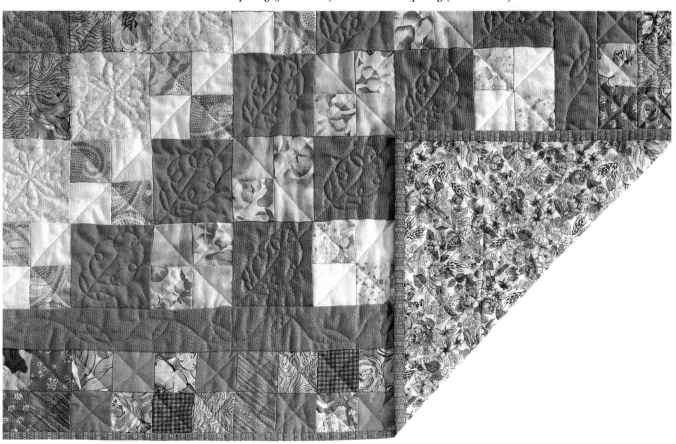

project. A quilt is usually a big project and can become cumbersome. You want to have a successful experience, so try different positions, cradling the machine with your arms, turning the machine to a different angle, etc., until you feel comfortable and ready to begin.

Two styles of quilting are done on the sewing machine, straight-line and free-motion. Straight-line quilting consists of all the straight lines on the quilt, including diagonals. All straight lines are quilted first. Use a walking foot for straight-line quilting. Keep your hands on the quilt at all times during straight-line quilting to control the top layer and the fullness.

In free-motion quilting, an open darning foot is required so that you can work around curves and to make intricate designs such as wreaths, cables, and stipple quilting. Lower the feed dog on your sewing machine,

bring the bobbin thread to the top side, and take small stitches in place to form a knot. Cut the thread tail. Start with the designs in the center of the quilt. Move the quilt around the curved designs.

1. Thread your machine either with cotton thread on both the top and bobbin or nylon on top and cotton in the bobbin. Attach a walking foot that is designed for your sewing machine.

2. Stitch around the entire quilt, ¼″ from the edges. This is an important step, as it protects the edges and prevents flaring and stretching.

3. Roll the quilt to expose the area to be quilted. Make sure there is ample surface area around your sewing machine to support the weight and bulk of the quilt. Do not allow the quilt to hang down, as the weight will cause stretching and distortion. If appropriate for your pattern, stitch

the quilt in quarters, horizontally and vertically, as shown.

4. To begin stitching, take two to three stitches forward and then two or three backstitches. With the needle in the up position, raise the presser foot and pull the bobbin thread to the top. Then cut the thread tail. Continue stitching. End the stitching line with two or three backstitches, and cut the threads.

✄ *HELPFUL HINT*: The walking foot is appropriate for all straight-line stitching, whereas an open darning foot works best for all free-form quilting.

5. Quilt one area at a time; unroll and re-roll to expose another area as necessary, until the entire quilt is completed.

6. Remove the safety pins.

You are ready to go to Chapter 7 and finish your quilt.

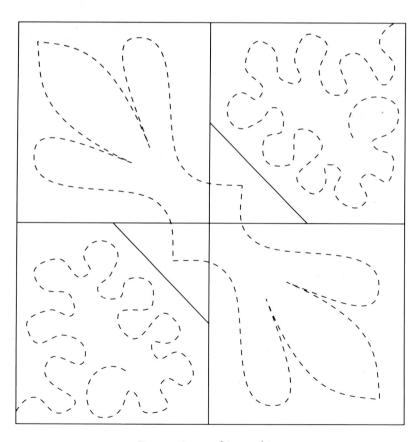

Free-motion machine quilting

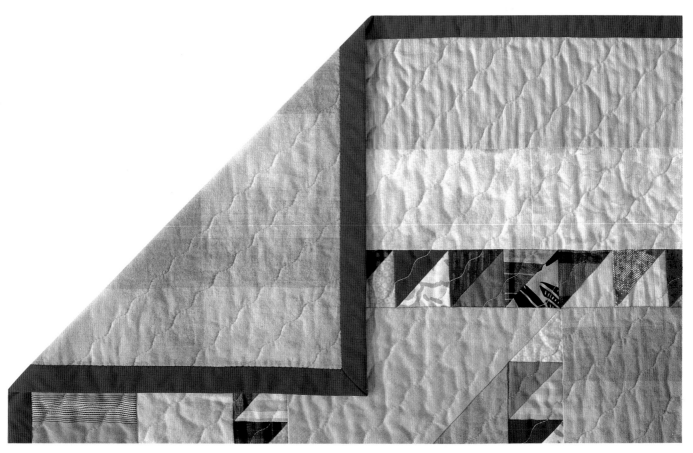

Above: Machine quilting (Sawtooth), *Below: Machine quilting* (Jewel Box)

Chapter 7
▼▼▼

BINDING

The binding is an important finishing touch to your quilt. We cannot caution you too much about this final phase—preparing the quilt edge, making accurate seams, cutting the continuous strip, and forming a miter at the corners. We suggest using a double-folded continuous strip, cut on the straight of the grain, either crosswise or lengthwise. This method is favored over the continuous bias strip for the quilts in this book because it stretches less while you are sewing it to the quilt, and it prevents flaring around the edges. We do, however, use bias strips for quilts with curved, scalloped, or zigzag edges.

▶ PREPARATION FOR BINDING

Before attaching the binding strips, it is important to trim the excess batting and backing, straighten the edges, and check to see that corners are at true 90° angles. Quilting may cause distortion along the edges of the quilt.

1. With the right side up, lay the quilt on a flat surface. Smooth it.

2. Slip the cutting board under that portion of your quilt to be trimmed. Then use the rotary cutter and wide plastic ruler to straighten the edges,

removing excess batting and backing. If you will be attaching a narrow ¼″ binding, trim the batting and backing even with the edge of the quilt top. However, if you prefer a wider binding, you must allow enough batting and backing to give support to the binding strip and prevent it from rippling. See the chart on page 154 to determine the required extension.

3. Continue to trim around the remaining edges of the quilt.

4. Use your wide plastic ruler to see that the corners are accurate 90° angles.

▶ ATTACHING A SLEEVE

A tube of fabric called a sleeve is often sewn to the back of a quilt. The sleeve is helpful for hanging your quilt on a rod or quilt shelf that has a wooden dowel. Also, if you want to display your quilt in a show, a sleeve is

usually required. This is a good time to attach a sleeve, because the raw edges can be concealed by the binding. The sleeve can be made from any fabric; leftover lengths of backing or border fabric work well, or even a piece of muslin.

1. Cut a 6½″-wide strip of fabric. The length is the measurement of the side of the quilt that will receive the sleeve.

2. Fold the short ends ¼″ to the wrong side and press. Fold over again ¼″ and press. Then stitch along the folded ends.

3. With the right side facing out, fold the piece of fabric in half lengthwise. Press to set the crease along the folded edge.

4. With the raw edges even with the raw edge of the quilt, lay the sleeve on the backside of the quilt. Pin to secure all layers.

5. Stitch the sleeve to the edge of the quilt, stitching through all layers, just shy of ¼″. The sleeve will not

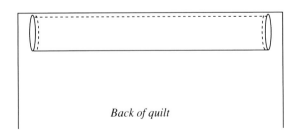

Back of quilt

Step 5

extend all the way to the ends, to allow for attaching binding strips.

6. Hand slipstitch the folded edge of the sleeve to the quilt, being careful to stitch *only* through the backing fabric.

▶ BINDING STRIPS

1. Measure around the edge of your quilt. Add 6″ to this measurement.

2. The fabric you are using for the binding may determine the direction you wish to cut it. For example, some directional prints are more pleasing if cut lengthwise, following the printed pattern; other fabrics are just fine cut on the crosswise grain. Determine how wide you would like your finished binding to be. Refer to the following chart for strip width measurements. The combined length of the binding strips must equal the figure determined in Step 1.

FINISHED WIDTH OF BINDING	CUT WIDTH OF STRIPS	BATTING AND BACKING EXTENSION
¼″	1¾″	none
⅜″	2¼″	⅛″
½″	2¾″	¼″
¾″	3¾″	½″
⅞″	4¼″	⅝″

3. Join the strips together, as shown, to make one continuous strip.

4. With the right side facing out, fold the strip in half lengthwise and press. Apply spray sizing to give stability and set the crease.

▶ ATTACHING BINDING STRIPS

This binding method creates miters on both the front and back sides at each corner. You want to avoid placing a seam joining strips at a corner, since it would cause additional bulk. To avoid this, make a trial run with the binding strip around the edge of the quilt to determine an

appropriate starting point along one of the sides.

1. With their right sides facing and cut edges even, lay the binding strip on the quilt. Then fold the starting end of the binding strip at a 45° angle, as shown.

2. Starting 3″ from the beginning of the binding strip, place pins to secure the strip to the quilt up to within ¼″ of the corner. Then stitch the binding to the quilt ¼″ from the edge of the quilt top, as shown. ✂ *HELPFUL HINT*: A walking foot on your sewing machine helps to keep the binding strip straight while sewing.

3. Continue stitching to within ¼″ of the corner. Then stop and back-stitch. Remove the quilt from the machine.

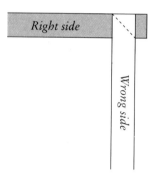

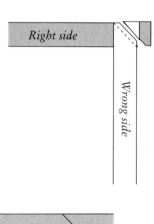

Step 3

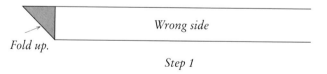

Fold up.

Step 1

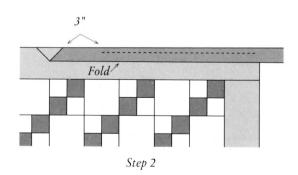

Fold

Step 2

▼

4. Lay the corner of the quilt on a flat surface and fold the binding strip away from the quilt, as shown.

5. Fold the binding strip toward you, the top folded edge even with the top edge of the quilt top, and the cut edges even with the side of the quilt, as shown. Pin to secure.

6. Starting at the folded edge of binding strip, stitch along the length to within ¼" of the next corner, as shown. Stop and backstitch.

7. Remove the quilt from the machine. Repeat Steps 4-6.

8. When you have come to within 4" of the starting point, stop and remove the quilt from the machine. Slip the end of the binding strip into the starting end, as shown. Trim any excess length if necessary. Pin to secure.

9. Stitch the final section of binding to the quilt.

10. Finger press the binding strip up and over the edge of the quilt to the back, folding the binding at the corners to form miters on both the front and back. Pin to hold in place on the back.

11. Use a hand slipstitch to secure the folded edge of the binding to the back of the quilt.

✄ *HELPFUL HINT*: If you prefer to attach the binding strip entirely by *machine*, you can first sew the binding strip to the *back*, following Steps 1-9.

Then fold it up and over the edge to the front. Topstitch ¹⁄₁₆" from the folded edge of the binding strip on the front, as shown.

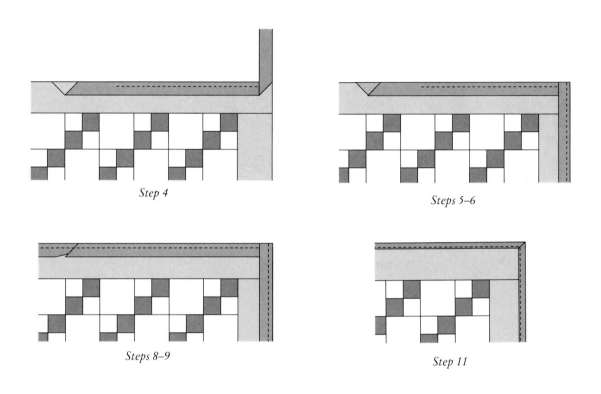

Step 4

Steps 5–6

Steps 8–9

Step 11

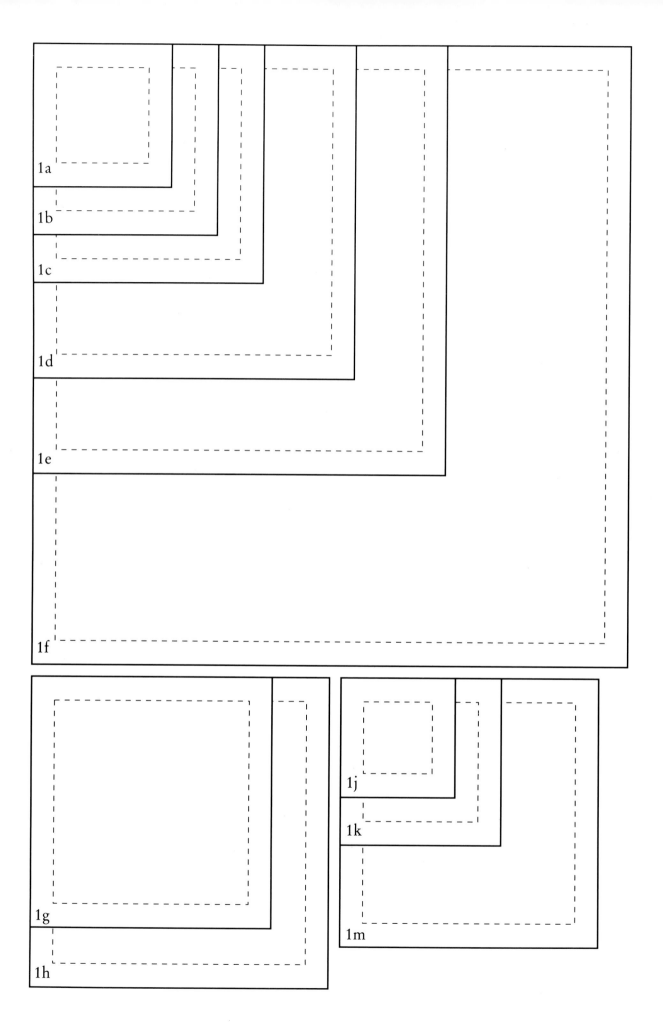

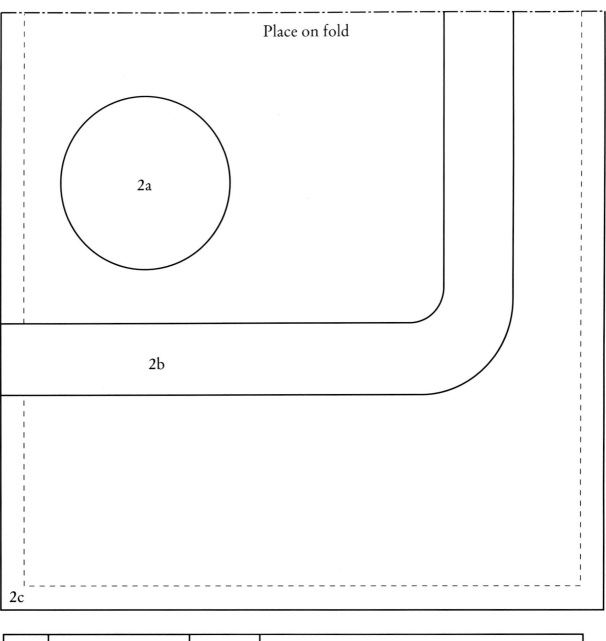

Place on fold

2a

2b

2c

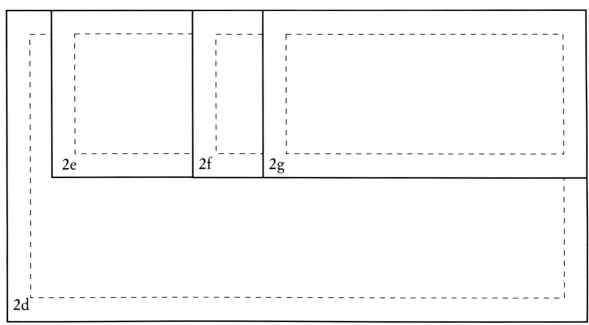

2e

2f

2g

2d

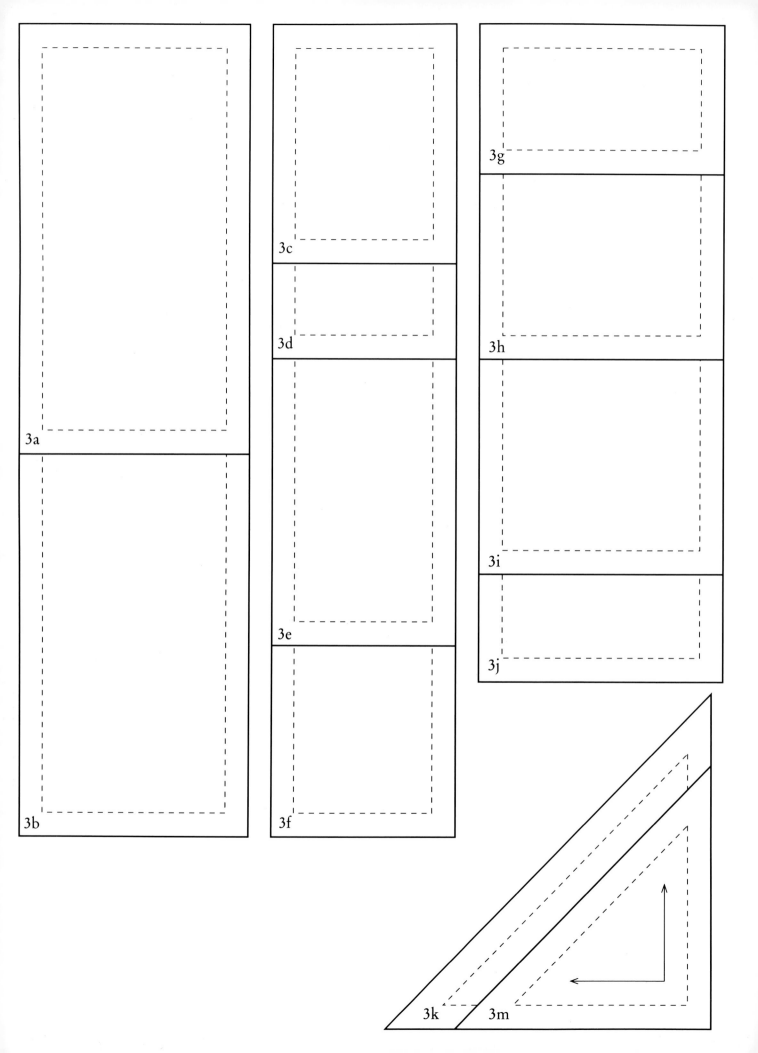

3a

3b

3c

3d

3e

3f

3g

3h

3i

3j

3k   3m

4a

4b

4c

4d

4e

4f

4g

4h

4i

4j

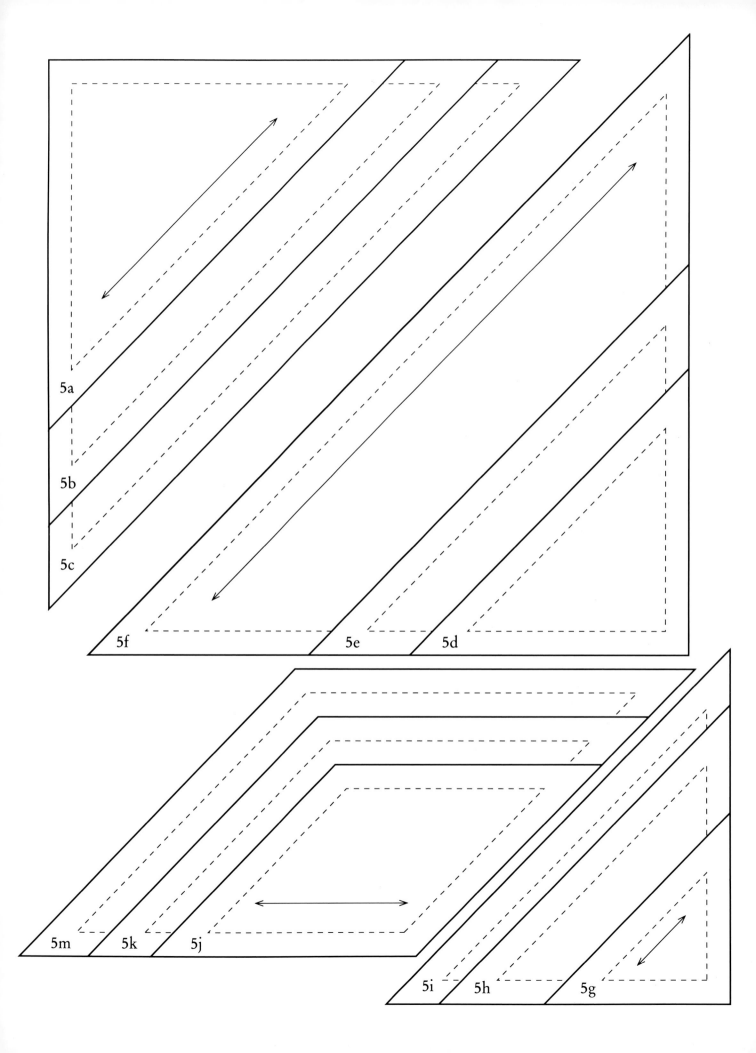

5a

5b

5c

5f   5e   5d

5m   5k   5j

5i   5h   5g

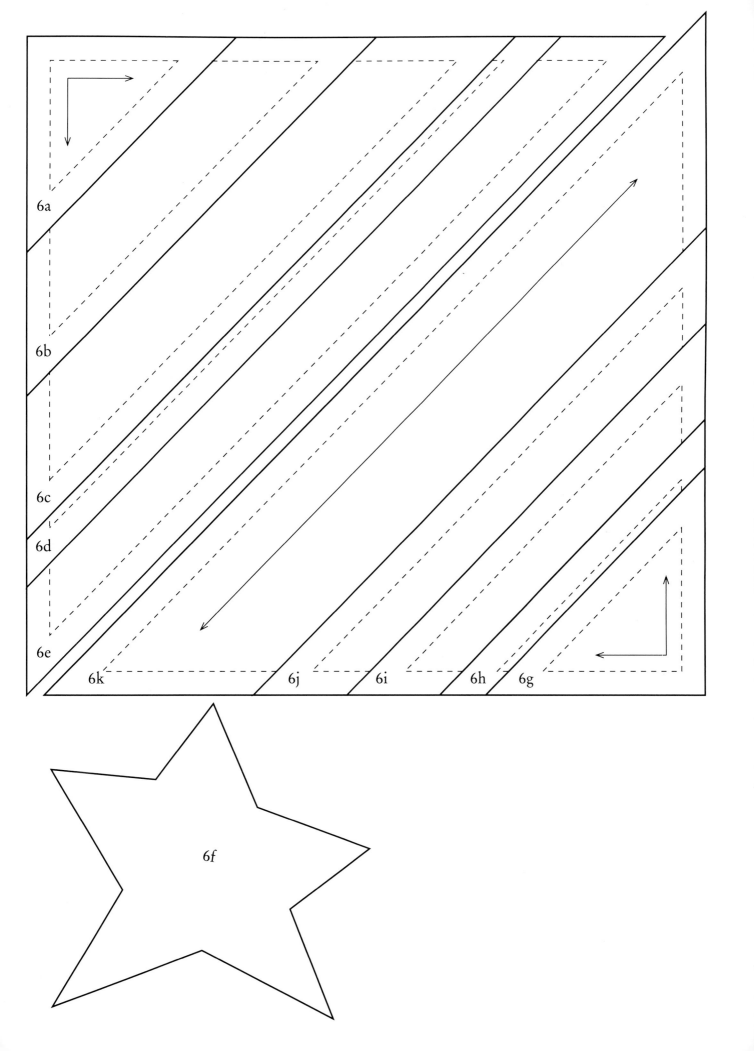

6a

6b

6c

6d

6e

6k   6j   6i   6h   6g

6f

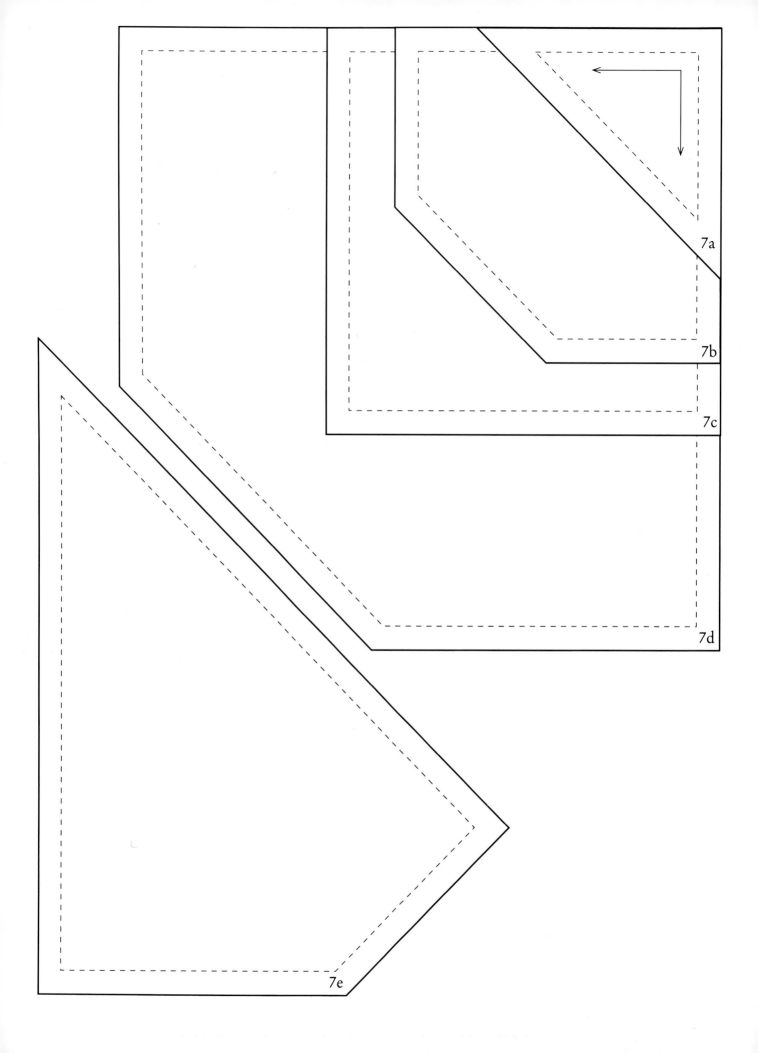

7a

7b

7c

7d

7e

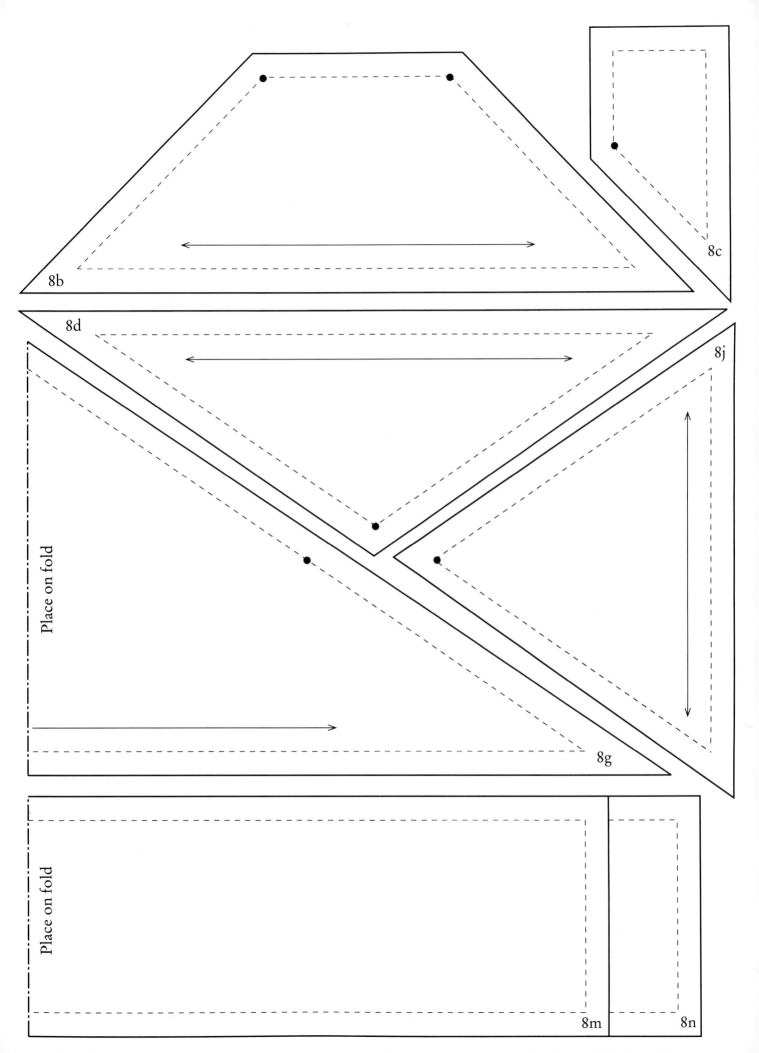

8c

8b

8d

8j

Place on fold

8g

Place on fold

8m

8n

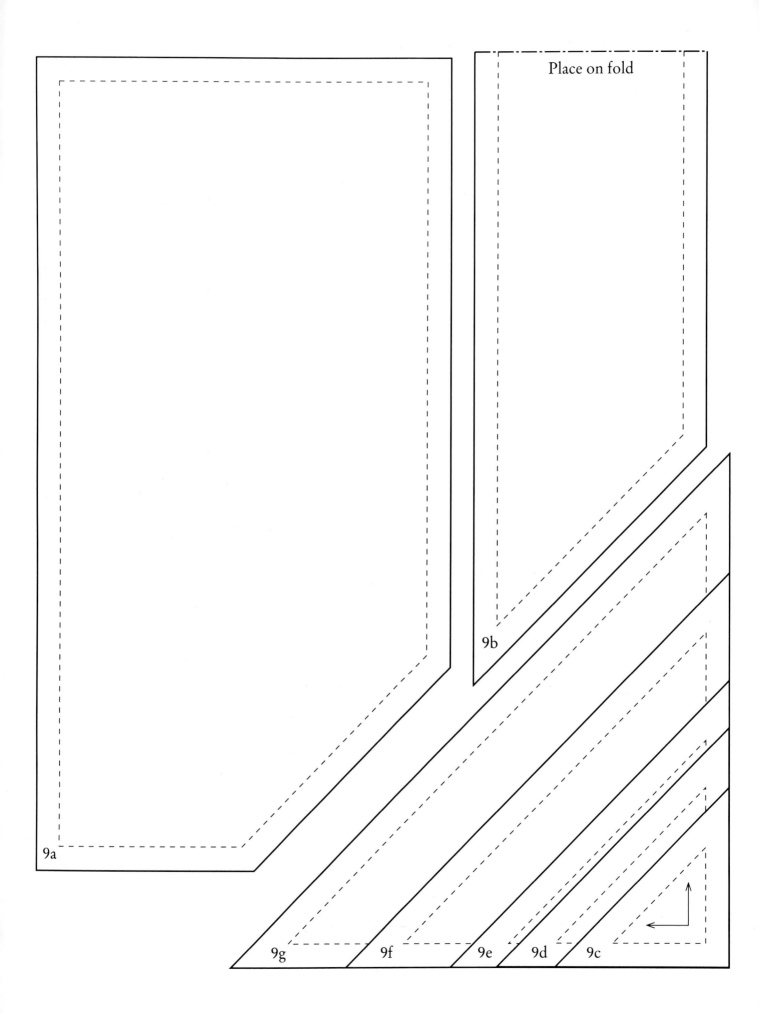

Place on fold

9a

9b

9g 9f 9e 9d 9c

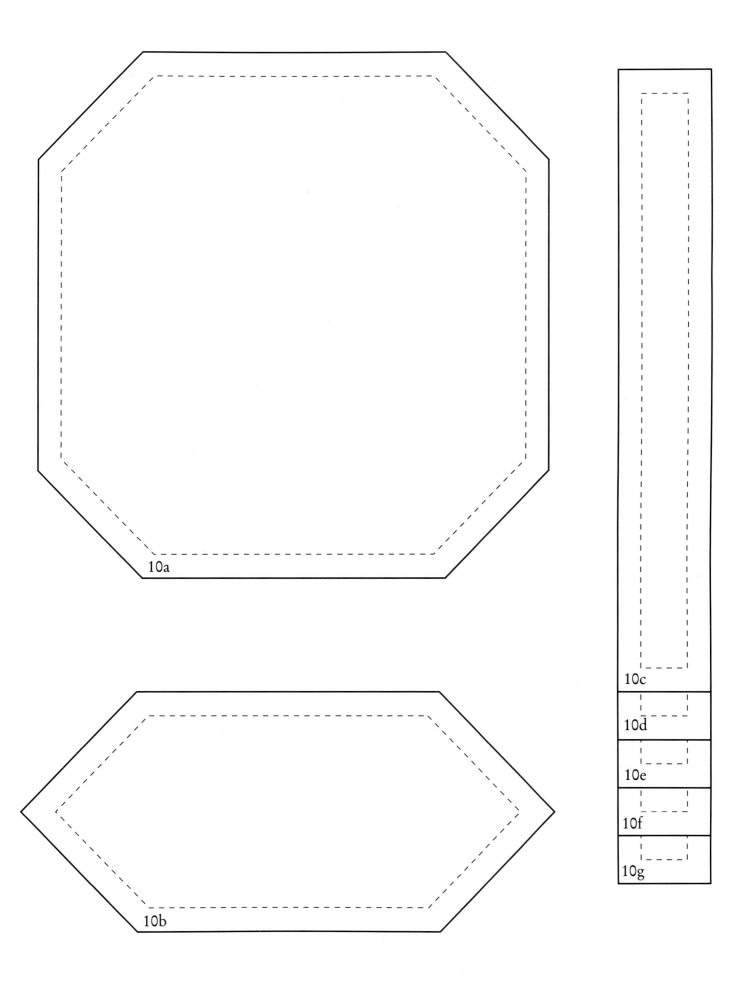

10a

10b

10c

10d

10e

10f

10g

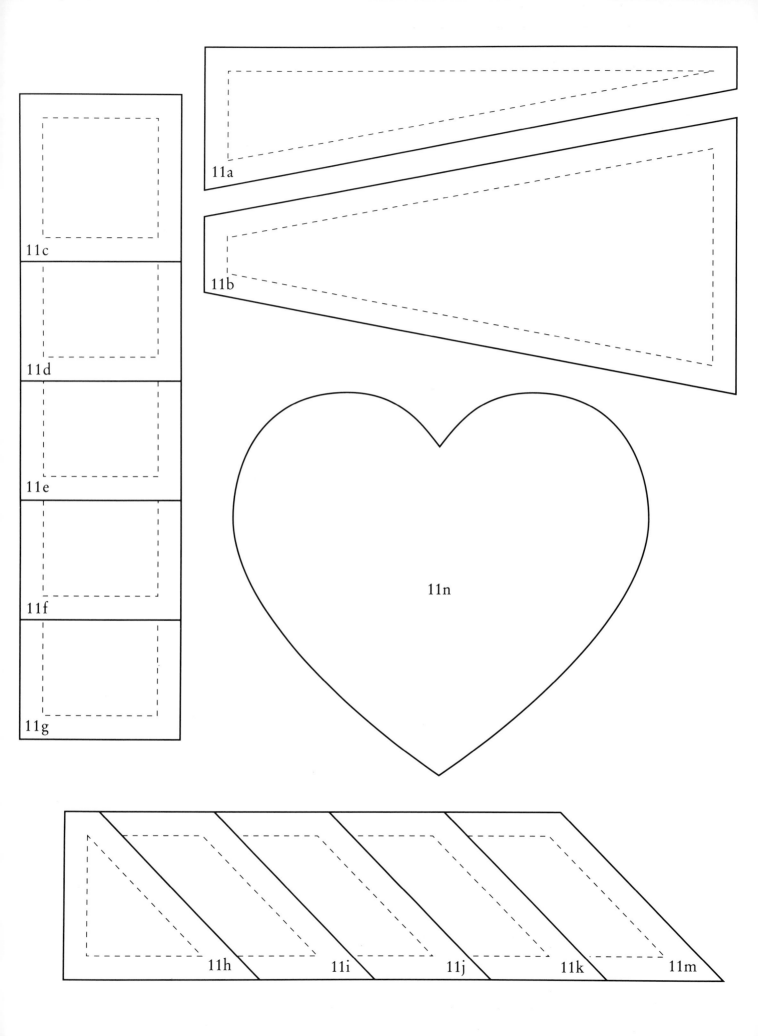

11c

11d

11e

11f

11g

11a

11b

11n

11h   11i   11j   11k   11m

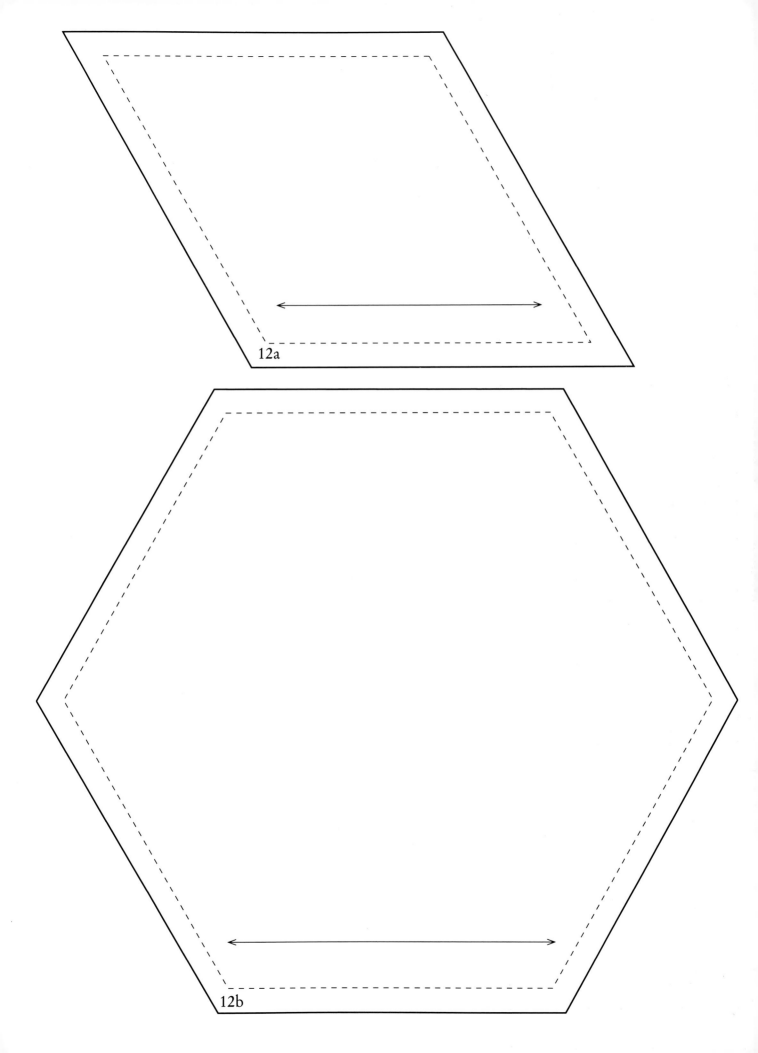

12a

12b

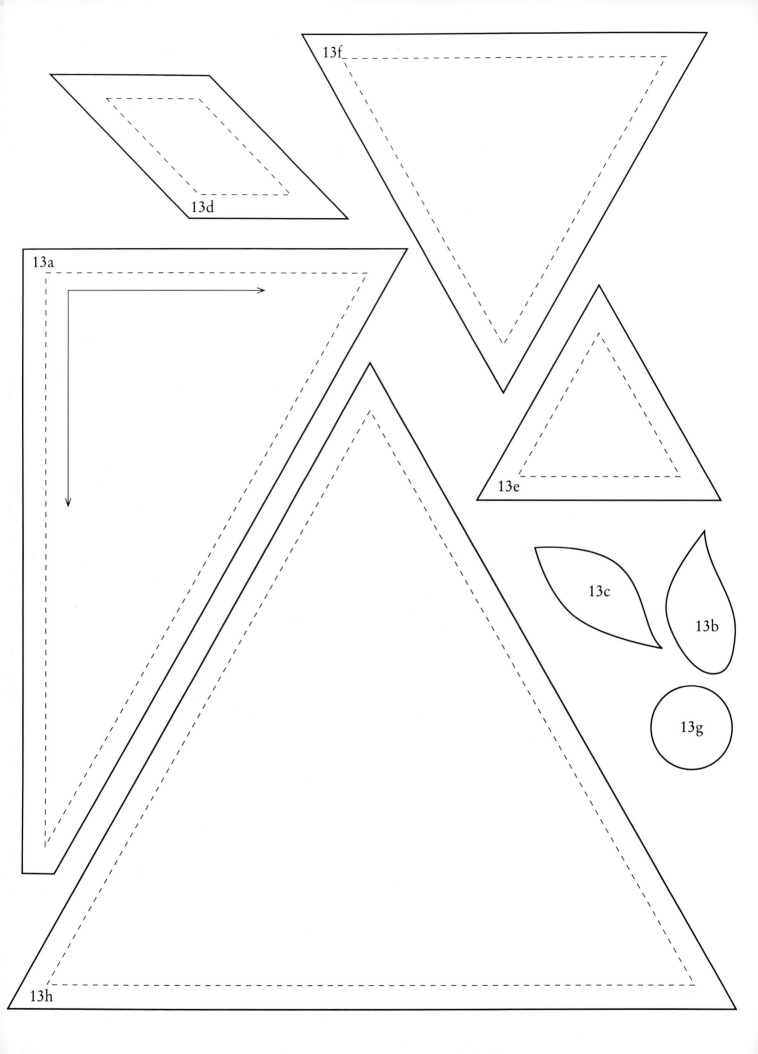

13f

13d

13a

13e

13c

13b

13g

13h

A	B
D	C

A

A B
D C

B

C

A | B
D | C

D

A B
D C

Machine quilting

Machine or hand quilting

Machine or hand quilting

▶ OTHER FINE QUILTING BOOKS
FROM C & T PUBLISHING

An Amish Adventure, Roberta Horton

Appliqué 12 Easy Ways!, Elly Sienkiewicz

The Art of Silk Ribbon Embroidery, Judith Montano

Baltimore Album Quilts, Historic Notes and Antique Patterns, Elly Sienkiewicz

Baltimore Beauties and Beyond (2 Volumes), Elly Sienkiewicz

The Best From Gooseberry Hill, Patterns for Stuffed Animals and Dolls, Kathy Pace

A Celebration of Hearts, Jean Wells and Marina Anderson

Christmas Traditions From the Heart, Margaret Peters

Crazy Quilt Handbook, Judith Montano

Crazy Quilt Odyssey, Judith Montano

Design a Baltimore Album Quilt!, Elly Sienkiewicz

Dimensional Appliqué—Baskets, Blooms & Borders, Elly Sienkiewicz

Friendship's Offering, Susan McKelvey

Heirloom Machine Quilting, Harriet Hargrave

Imagery on Fabric, Jean Ray Laury

Isometric Perspective, Katie Pasquini-Masopust

Landscapes & Illusions, Joen Wolfrom

The Magical Effects of Color, Joen Wolfrom

Mastering Machine Appliqué, Harriet Hargrave

Memorabilia Quilting, Jean Wells

NSA Series: Bloomin' Creation, Jean Wells

NSA Series: Holiday Magic, Jean Wells

NSA Series: Hometown, Jean Wells

NSA Series: Hearts, Fans, Folk Art, Jean Wells

Pattern Play, Doreen Speckmann

PQME Series: Milky Way Quilt, Jean Wells

PQME Series: Nine-Patch Quilt, Jean Wells

PQME Series: Pinwheel Quilt, Jean Wells

PQME Series: Stars & Hearts Quilt, Jean Wells

Recollections, Judith Montano

Stitching Free: Easy Machine Pictures, Shirley Nilsson

Story Quilts, Mary Mashuta

Three-Dimensional Design, Katie Pasquini

A Treasury of Quilt Labels, Susan McKelvey

Visions: The Art of the Quilt, Quilt San Diego

Whimsical Animals, Miriam Gourley

For more information write for a free catalog from
C & T Publishing
P.O. Box 1456
Lafayette, CA 94549
(1-800-284-1114)